SAINT-SAËNS

Mon cœur s'ouvre à ta voix Comme s'ouvrent les fleurs

C. Saint-Saëns

SAINT-SAËNS

BY ARTHUR HERVEY

Select Bibliographies Reprint Series

BOOKS FOR LIBRARIES PRESS
FREEPORT, NEW YORK

First Published 1922
Reprinted 1969

STANDARD BOOK NUMBER:
8369-5045-3

LIBRARY OF CONGRESS CATALOG CARD NUMBER:
70-94271

PRINTED IN THE UNITED STATES OF AMERICA

TO

MY WIFE

PREFACE

ON October 9, 1920, Camille Saint-Saëns celebrated his eighty-fifth birthday. A career
commencing in the early days of childhood
and concerned with well-nigh every branch of
musical activity is indeed quite unique.

One reads with astonishment that his piano-playing
in a drawing-room at the age of four years and seven
months was sufficiently remarkable to be thought worthy
of a notice in the *Moniteur Universel*. Over eighty years
have gone by since then !

When Saint-Saëns was a boy, Mendelssohn, Chopin,
and Schumann were alive ; Meyerbeer was the supreme
master of opera ; Berlioz was striving hard, and not too
successfully, to obtain recognition ; Wagner and Verdi
were at the beginning of their glorious careers ; Gounod,
having lately won the Prix de Rome, was earning his
livelihood as an organist ; Dumas, Balzac, Victor Hugo,
Georges Sand, were at the zenith of their fame ; Louis
Philippe, the citizen king, ruled over the French.
Between then and now, what a difference !

Saint-Saëns has lived through these times, and if he
felt inclined to refer to them would be amply justified
in applying to himself the words of the poet, " Quorum
pars magna fui."

He has acquired universal fame as a composer, pianist, and organist. He has been closely associated with the great movement of the age, and has been intimately acquainted with some of the most celebrated artists. He has been able to note the gradual changes that have occurred in the art he himself has illustrated so admirably, and to realize the enormous advance made by the French public in the general appreciation of music. During these long years he has been able to witness the birth and development of many a career flourishing side by side with his own.

Saint-Saëns was one of the chief protagonists of that period extending from 1870 to the end of the century which constituted a veritable Renaissance of French music illustrated by a galaxy of remarkable composers. Berlioz was dead, Auber had died during the Commune, whilst Ambroise Thomas and Gounod had already made their reputation. Those who came prominently to the fore during that brilliant period in addition to Saint-Saëns were César Franck, Reyer, Lalo, Bizet (whose career was destined to be so prematurely cut short), Delibes, Massenet, Guiraud, Paladilhe, Widor, Fauré, Chabrier, and, during the latter part, Vincent d'Indy, Alfred Bruneau, Debussy, Charpentier, amongst others. Concerning the younger composers who have appeared since, and they are many, it is yet too early to speak. Many of them are imbued with high artistic ideals, and will doubtless do honour to their country and to themselves.

At the present moment, when great changes are being effected in every province of life, and when the " old order " is rapidly passing away, it is not surprising that the art of music should be correspondingly affected.

Rubinstein many years ago expressed himself convinced that " music not only reflects the individuality and spiritual emotion of the composer," but is also " the echo and refrain of the age, the historical events, the state of society, culture, etc., in which it is written." Were he alive now he would doubtless find ample corroboration of his theory, for the present unsettled state of the world is certainly reflected in much of the music of to-day.

A fresh departure seems to have taken place in music during the last few years. It is still too soon to hazard an opinion as to where this may lead, but a tendency among some of the younger composers of different nations appears to point to a thorough negation of the fundamental principles of music hitherto more or less generally accepted. The desire, praiseworthy in itself, of avoiding conventionality, has led to fearsome experiments in sound. Whereas in the past, respect for formalism was pushed too far and barred the way to the free development of music, the so-called modernists are now going to the other extreme and, throwing all precedent to the winds, are seemingly endeavouring to create an entirely new language of sound, the adoption of which would necessitate the scrapping of all the masterpieces of the past. This appears to be a retrograde movement rather than an advance, for it can only lead straight back to the chaotic conditions that prevailed before mankind was civilized and able to appreciate what is understood as music. A similar tendency has long been apparent in the sister art of painting, but the efforts of futurists, independents, and cubists have not yet succeeded in corrupting the taste of art lovers or in destroying the cult of the great masters of pictorial art. It is highly unlikely that the discordant attempts of the musical futurists will meet with any more success or do any permanent harm, except to themselves.

It is well at such a moment to ponder over the magnificent example set by an artist like Saint-Saëns who, during his long and varied career, has always known how to steer clear of exaggeration, and who has shown conclusively by the freedom with which he has treated different forms of music that imagination is not hampered by knowledge, that true progress does not consist necessarily in abandoning all the traditions of the past, but that these should not, on the other hand, prevent a composer from cultivating an entire independence in the expression of his thoughts. It is by remaining faithful to these principles that the great French composer has succeeded in attaining the position he has long held in the estimation of all true lovers of music.

ARTHUR HERVEY.

Mon cher [...]

soyez assez bon

pour accueillir

Monsieur Henry

que j'ai rencontré

à Londres et qui

se rend à Weimar

tout exprès pour

travailler sous votre direction. Je pense que vous n'aurez pas à vous repentir de vous en charger car il est animé des meilleures intentions.

J'ai vu que vous aviez encore donné _Dalila_ je vous en remercie; je vous le dis si vous avez pu jouer

FACSIMILE OF AUTOGRAPH LETTER FROM M. SAINT-SAËNS

la princesse Jeanne [-] — s'il qu'il en a été
question.

Mes respects à
votre charmante et excellente
amie qui a été si bonne
pour moi.

Mille amitiés

C. Saint-Saëns

AUTHOR'S NOTE

THE present volume is the first written in the English language entirely devoted to the life and works of Saint-Saëns. For some of the dates and for certain biographical details mentioned in the first chapter the author is indebted to the excellent monograph on Saint-Saëns by M. Jean Bonnerot as well as to articles by the composer himself. The autograph letter reproduced herein was given to the present writer many years ago as an introduction to Eduard Lassen, the gifted composer, at that time Court Capellmeister at Weimar. It was Eduard Lassen who conducted the initial performance of *Samson and Delilah* at Weimar. This opera was originally entitled *Dalila*, as will be seen by the letter now reproduced.

A. H.

CONTENTS

LIST OF ILLUSTRATIONS

SAINT-SAËNS

CHAPTER I

BIOGRAPHICAL

THE birth of Charles Camille Saint-Saëns, to give him his full name, took place in Paris at No. 3 Rue du Jardinet, on October 9, 1835.

His father, who was employed in a Government office, was of good Norman stock and had left his birthplace near Dieppe to settle in Paris, where he had fallen in love with a young girl named Clémence Collin, then residing in the Rue Mignon with her aunt Mme Masson, and whom he married in 1834. This union was blessed the following year by the birth of a son, the subject of the present volume.

A few weeks later, on December 31, the exact anniversary of his marriage day, the father succumbed at the early age of thirty-seven, a victim to the scourge of consumption. Mme Masson, the aunt of the young widow, had lost her own husband a few months previously, and the two bereaved women now concentrated all their affection upon the little child whose tiny frame was already said to contain germs of the same dread disease which had carried off his father. Fresh country air having been prescribed by the faculty, the baby was

I

put to nurse at Corbeil for the two following years, at the end of which he was brought back to Paris.

The tender care lavished upon him by his mother and his great-aunt brought its reward, for the little fellow's health rapidly improved, and very soon he displayed unmistakable signs of an abnormal musical instinct. In his case, unlike that of several other famous composers, his musical precocity was hailed with delight by those whom he termed his two mothers, and Mme Masson lost no time in teaching him his notes.

He has related himself how at the age of two he liked to listen to various sounds, such as the creaking of doors and the striking of clocks. His great pleasure was what he terms "the symphony of the kettle, an enormous kettle which was placed every morning in front of the fire." Seating himself by this, the little fellow waited with "a passionate curiosity for its first murmurs, its slow crescendo so full of surprises and the appearance of a microscopic hautboy the sound of which rose little by little until the water had reached boiling point."

From the same unimpeachable source we gather that he was then learning to read, that when only two years and six months old he was placed in front of a small piano, that instead of striking the keyboard in a haphazard manner, as children do at that age, he "touched the notes one after the other, and only left them when the sound had evaporated."

Having learnt the names of the notes, the individual sounds became so fixed in his brain that when the piano was being tuned he was able, to the general astonishment, while playing in the adjoining room, to name correctly each note as it was struck.

So unmistakable a musical precocity recalls that of

Mozart and of Liszt. Like the above masters, Saint-Saëns seems to have experienced little difficulty in mastering the rudiments of music. The astonishing progress made by this veritably surprising child led to his playing the piano part in one of Beethoven's violin sonatas before a select audience in a drawing-room at the age of four years and seven months, a fact which was duly chronicled in a eulogious article which appeared in the *Moniteur Universel* of August 1, 1840.

During the next few years, side by side with his musical studies, his general education was being actively pursued, and he seems to have exhibited an equal facility in acquiring a knowledge of Latin, geometry, and other subjects.

When seven years old, he received lessons on the piano from Stamaty, who was reputed to have been Kalkbrenner's best pupil, and some months later he was initiated into the mysteries of harmony by an erudite professor named Maleden.

Not content with striving to interpret the works of others, the little musician was also endeavouring to create on his own account, and he was not even afraid to try his prentice hand on the composition of a sonata.

About this time he awakened the admiration of the famous painter Ingres, who presented him with a medallion representing the profile of Mozart and bearing this composer's signature, under which he added the words : " To my young friend M. Saint-Saëns, charming interpreter of the divine artist." Another valuable present offered to the boy by an admirer consisted of a copy of the full score of Mozart's *Don Juan* richly bound in red morocco.

The moment arrived when, at the age of ten, he was

considered sufficiently advanced by his master Stamaty to display his pianistic talent in public ; so, after two preliminary matinées, he gave a concert at the Salle Pleyel on May 6, 1846, which obtained an immense success, the young musician being hailed as another Mozart. The serious and exacting task accomplished by the youthful artist may be gauged by the programme which included two Concertos, one by Mozart and the other by Beethoven, a sonata by Hummel, besides a Prelude and Fugue by Bach, and pieces by Handel and Kalkbrenner, all of which were played from memory.

After having made so sensational a début the boy was very wisely withdrawn from the deleterious atmosphere of public life and kept to his studies. With the exception of occasional appearances in public, he devoted himself to the study of the organ at the Conservatoire under Benoist, and later on, in 1850, he joined the class for Composition presided over by Halévy. In 1852 he unsuccessfully competed for the Prix de Rome.

Saint-Saëns, who had commenced his musical career in so auspicious a manner, was now encountering his first rebuff. More disappointments were destined to follow, but a characteristic trait in his nature, one which has asserted itself throughout his life, is the determination never to accept defeat nor to allow ill-success to discourage him from further effort. So during that same year he set bravely to work, and carried off a prize offered by the Société Sainte Cécile with an Ode in honour of the patron saint of the Society.

This initial success was succeeded by another the following year, when the same Society, directed by Seghers, produced the young composer's first Symphony.

The honour was all the greater as, fearing that his youth might prejudice the members of the Committee against him, he sent in his Symphony anonymously on the advice of Seghers, who pretended that the score had reached him from Germany without bearing any composer's name. When the work was played it produced a very favourable impression and evoked the praise of Berlioz and Gounod.

In December 1852 he had been appointed organist of the Church of Saint Merry, a post which he retained for some five years, during which he continued adding to his compositions and writing works such as the Quintet in A minor and another Symphony in F which has never been published. About this time he wrote a Mass and dedicated it to the Abbé Gabriel, curé of the above church, who was so pleased that he rewarded his young organist by taking him on a short visit to Rome, where he was able to hear the famous singers of the Sixtine Chapel.

A great stroke of luck occurred to him in 1858, when he was appointed organist of the Church of the Madeleine in succession to Lefébure Wély, who vacated the post that year.

As the Madeleine is the most fashionable church in Paris, it may be imagined that the competition to preside there in the organ-loft was very keen. Saint-Saëns was fortunate enough to have a good friend in the Abbé Deguerry, the curé of the church, who was destined to meet with such a tragic fate in 1871 as one of the hostages shot by the Communists. Thanks to this excellent man, the young artist obtained the much-coveted post, which brought him in an income of 3000 francs a year, and which he retained until 1877, when he was suc-

ceeded by his friend Théodore Dubois, who in turn
had as his successor Gabriel Fauré.

Two years later, in 1860, after the death of Niedermeyer, Saint-Saëns became a professor in the Institute
bearing this musician's name, and remained there three
years, during which time he numbered among his pupils
the composers Gabriel Fauré and André Messager, the
organists Eugène Gigout and Edouard Marlois. The
last-named, an exceptionally gifted musician, settled in
London, and was gradually becoming known as pianist,
organist, and conductor, when he caught a severe chill
and died in the winter of 1881 at about thirty-three years
of age. Saint-Saëns held him in high esteem and was
much affected by his premature death.

Although his position was by this time well established,
Saint-Saëns made another attempt, in 1864, to win the
Prix de Rome. A second time was fate against him, and
the prize was adjudged to one Victor Sieg, whose sub-
sequent career did not justify the choice of the jury of
the Conservatoire, and who, after having been organist
and inspector of singing for the city of Paris, died in
1890. So much for the value of academic verdicts!

Three years later Saint-Saëns was to be compensated
for this failure by being unanimously adjudged the
victor over more than a hundred other musicians in a
competition instituted by the Imperial Government on
the occasion of the International Exhibition of 1867
for the best setting of a cantata entitled *Les Noces de
Prométhée*. Berlioz, who was on the jury, in a letter
to his friend Ferrand, expressed his delight at the success
of "his young friend Camille Saint-Saëns, one of the
greatest musicians of our epoch."

It will be realized that the appreciation of composers

like Berlioz, Gounod, and Liszt was something for a
young musician to value. Another illustrious admirer
was to be added to the above in no less a person than the
redoubtable Richard Wagner, whose acquaintance Saint-
Saëns had made at the time of the memorable production
of *Tannhäuser* at the Paris Opéra in 1861, and who was
astounded at the ease with which his most complicated
scores were interpreted then and there on the piano
by the gifted young musician. On one occasion, at
Bayreuth, the great Richard in toasting his health is
said to have dubbed him the greatest living French
composer.

During the early days of his career Saint-Saëns came
into contact with Anton Rubinstein. In a delightful
article, republished in the volume entitled *Portraits et
Souvenirs*, he has related the manner in which he first
became acquainted with the great Russian, how this
acquaintance rapidly developed into a fast friendship,
and how Rubinstein asked him to conduct the orchestra
at certain concerts he proposed to give in Paris. After
eight of these concerts had taken place, Rubinstein one
day said to Saint-Saëns that he had never yet conducted
an orchestra himself in Paris and would like to do so.
The matter was speedily settled, and the concert fixed
to take place in three weeks' time. In this short interval
Saint-Saëns undertook to compose a piano Concerto
for the occasion, which he did, and played the solo
part himself, Rubinstein directing the orchestra.

The Concerto in question is the one in G minor,
No. 2, Op. 22, which was published in the same year of
its composition and production, 1868, and has become
one of the most popular works of its kind, a battle-horse
in the répertoire of every pianist.

The phenomenal rapidity with which Saint-Saëns composed and scored this famous Concerto proves the spontaneity of his inspiration and explains how he has been able to produce such an enormous quantity of music, possible only to one who has his ideas absolutely under control. The probability is that he must have had the plan of the music in his head at the time, as the manual labour of writing it down, let alone that of mastering the solo part, would involve many hours of hard work. He says himself that, owing to this hurry, he did not play the solo part well, but that the Scherzo at once took the fancy of the audience.

The triumphs obtained by Saint-Saëns in the concert-room had brought his name to the fore, his great merits had been recognized in musical circles, and the bestowal of the decoration of the Legion of Honour, in 1868, had set the official stamp on his successes.

He had not, however, yet succeeded in reaching that larger public which in France can only be approached through the medium of the stage. If this is still the case at the present time, it was far more so in the early days of Saint-Saëns' career, when concerts were fewer in number and their programmes were mainly devoted to the works of classical masters. It was natural, therefore, that he should have desired to show his capability of writing operas as well as symphonies.

The difficulties encountered by Saint-Saëns in his efforts to obtain a hearing on the operatic boards have been related by himself in his article " Histoire d'un Opéra-Comique." The very successes he had obtained as a composer of symphonic works went against him. What could a writer of symphonies know about operas ? The fact of his being an organist and a pianist made matters worse, particularly the last of these qualifications. " Bizet," he writes, " who played the piano admirably, never dared to play in public for fear of aggravating his situation."

A fair Princess of artistic tendencies having been asked to interest herself in Saint-Saëns answered, " What ? Is he not content with his position ? He plays the organ at the Madeleine and the piano in my house. Is that not sufficient for him ? "

At last he was entrusted with a libretto, that of *Le Timbre d'Argent*, and in 1865 had sketched out the music of the work, which was in five acts. For many weary months Saint-Saëns tried in vain to have his opera produced. Then came the Franco-German War in 1870, followed by the fall of the Second Empire, and music in France necessarily came to a standstill for a while.

During the tragic days of the siege of Paris, Saint-Saëns did his duty as a patriot and donned the uniform of a soldier of the National Guard. At intervals he contrived to find time to devote to his art, and the well-known " Marche Héroïque," dedicated to the memory of his friend, the painter Henri Regnault, killed in a battle near Paris, belongs to this period.

Before the war he had thought out a plan of giving concerts for the sake of trying to interest the public in the works of French composers. This idea was further developed after the siege of Paris, and led to the foundation of the Société Nationale de Musique. The Society in question, however, had scarcely come into existence when its labours were interrupted by the horrors of the Commune, and Saint-Saëns had to leave Paris and take refuge in London, where he found Gounod and other compatriots, exiles like himself. Thus began his long association with this country.

He made his first appearance in London in 1871, at one of the excellent concerts of the Musical Union directed by John Ella, pleasant reunions which were the means of furthering the cause of Chamber music and were attractively informal in character.

The Commune having been suppressed and quieter times prevailing, he was able to return to Paris. The period of the Renaissance of French music, in which Saint-Saëns was destined to play so prominent a part, was now at hand. The time had arrived when he was to be afforded the opportunity of bringing forth some of the finest fruits of his genius. Many of the works through which he is known best were written during the seventies, years notable for a practically unceasing creative activity on his part.

An ardent admirer of Liszt, he had been deeply impressed by this master's Symphonic Poems. His enthusiasm for these master-works had fired his imagination, and the idea of symphonically illustrating a given subject appealed greatly to his mind. " To many people," he wrote, " Programme music is a necessarily inferior *genre*. A quantity of things have been written on this subject that I find it impossible to understand. Is the music in itself good or bad ? Everything depends on this. Whether it be or not accompanied by a programme it will neither be better nor worse."

It was under the influence of these ideas that he came to write the exquisite *Rouet d'Omphale* (1871), the brilliant *Phaeton* (1873), the weird *Danse Macabre* (1874), the energetic *Jeunesse d'Hercule* (1876), works which occupy a permanent place in every concert répertoire.

The piano Concerto in C minor, No. 4, Op. 44, one of his finest works, and the oratorio *Le Déluge* belong to the same fruitful period.

Saint-Saëns was again in London in July 1874, when he appeared as pianist at one of the concerts of the Royal Philharmonic Society. This event is chronicled in the following paragraph from Mr. Myles Birket Foster's History of the Society : " The eminent French musician, M. Saint-Saëns, organist of the Madeleine, made his first appearance as pianist. He wrote, ' If my own Concerto alarms you, I will play Beethoven,' and added, as to choice of pianoforte, with true French *politesse* : ' I esteem Broadwood, I prefer Erard.' Apparently the Directors did show signs of alarm, as he played Beethoven's Concerto in G ! "

The Concerto of his own that Saint-Saëns mentioned was probably the well-known one in G minor, which he played at the Society's concert on July 2, 1879, the Directors of that season being evidently of a more venturesome disposition. On this same occasion he displayed his talent as an organist by performing a Prelude and Fugue of Bach.

During one of his visits to London about this time he met with an accident which might have had serious consequences. A fall through an open trapdoor resulted in his receiving injuries to his back from which he did not recover for some time. It so happened that he had promised to take part in an arrangement for eight hands of his own " Marche Héroïque " at a concert given by Sir Julius Benedict. Somehow or other he managed to get on to the platform and perform his part, but when it came to acknowledging the applause of the audience he found that he could not bend forward and bow, and so was forced to slide off the platform as best he could.

The operatic début of Saint-Saëns, a modest one, took place in 1872 at the Opéra-Comique Theatre with a one-act piece entitled *La Princesse Jaune*. His friend Bizet's *Djamileh* was produced in the course of the same year at the same theatre. Both works were ruthlessly criticized by the Press, and stated to be discordant, obscure, and what not. At that time Saint-Saëns had finished his opera *Le Timbre d'Argent*, but he had to wait until 1877 for this work to be produced at the Opéra National Lyrique, when a somewhat incoherent libretto prevented the music from obtaining more than a *succès d'estime*.

Compensation came to the composer at the close of the same year when, through the recommendation of Liszt, his now famous opera *Samson and Delilah*, originally known simply as *Dalila*, was produced for the first time on the stage at Weimar, achieving a success which was repeated when the work was given at Hamburg, Cologne, Prague, Dresden, and other towns.

It is scarcely conceivable that this now universally admired opera should not have been given in the composer's native land until 1890, over twelve years after its production at Weimar, and then not in Paris, but at Rouen! It was first heard in the French capital during the autumn of that year at the Eden Theatre. Performances followed at Lyons, Marseilles, Aix-les-Bains, Bordeaux, Toulouse, Nantes, Montpellier, Nice, Dijon, Florence, and Geneva. Eventually it was incorporated into the répertoire of the Paris Opéra, where it has remained ever since.

Owing to the ban against the performance of operas

founded on Biblical subjects which formerly existed in England, it was a long time before a stage representation of *Samson and Delilah* was allowed to be given in this country. It was first presented to the London public in the form of an oratorio at a Covent Garden promenade concert in 1893 under the direction of Sir Frederic, then Mr., Cowen. The performance in question took place under great difficulties, substitutes for the two artists originally cast for the name parts having to be secured at a few hours' notice. Nevertheless, the work created a marked impression, and this was intensified subsequently when it was given at the Queen's Hall. Its stage production at Covent Garden did not take place until the season of 1909.

The amount of work achieved by Saint-Saëns during the years that followed the Franco-German War was enormous. His pen was never idle, and one work was immediately succeeded by another.

It was in 1878 that he composed a Requiem, which was to be performed on May 22 that year on the anniversary of the death of a certain M. Libon. He is said to have taken only eight days to write this work. In any case it was ready for performance at the stated time. A few days later a terrible domestic tragedy occurred, which cast a deep gloom over the composer's life. The eldest of his two children, a little boy aged two and a half years, fell out of a window on the fourth floor and was killed. This tragic event was succeeded shortly afterwards by the death of his second son, a baby of seven months. It was only by throwing himself heart and soul into his work that the bereaved father was able to find some sort of solace to his overpowering grief.

Le Timbre d'Argent and *Samson et Dalila* having been produced, he had turned his attention again to the operatic stage, and had begun writing *Étienne Marcel*, an opera founded on a subject taken from the history of France. He completed this work in the course of that year, and it was produced for the first time at Lyons during the following winter.

In the summer of 1879 he came to England for the production of his cantata, *The Lyre and the Harp*, at the Birmingham festival. His impressions of the festival were noted in an extremely interesting article, republished in the volume entitled *Harmonie et Mélodie*. He expressed his admiration of the festival chorus in the following words : " I wish that those who consider the English devoid of musical feeling could hear the Birmingham choristers. Accuracy, precision in time and rhythm, finesse in the lights and shades, charm in the sonority—this wonderful chorus unites everything. If people who sing like this are not musicians, they do exactly what they would do if they were the best musicians in the world." He ends his article with a curious explanation of the position occupied in the affections of the English by Handel, who, he says, is the base of the oratorio, " the daily bread of every musical festival." He further attributes this to causes other than purely musical ones. " England," he writes, " has been sometimes Catholic, sometimes Protestant ; in reality, she could not be Protestant like the Germanic race, nor Catholic like the Latin races. England is Biblical, and the Old Testament holds in her religion a place almost equal to that which it holds in the Jewish religion. This explains the intensity of success of works such as *Israel in Egypt, Elijah, Solomon,* the subjects of which will never

M. SAINT-SAËNS, ABOUT 1879-80

have for the publics of the Continent the interest they
have for the English."

The great sympathy, one might say the feeling of
attachment, exhibited by Saint-Saëns towards England
has often been expressed in print. It was from the
history of England that the subject of his next opera
was taken. The libretto of this, the first of his dramatic
works to be produced at the Paris Grand Opéra, was
concocted by Léonce Détroyat and Armand Sylvestre
round the personality of our bluff King Hal.

The composer has related how, in order to realize
the physiognomy of the epoch, he had profited by his
friendship with the librarian of the Royal library at
Buckingham Palace to look through the musical treasures
of the past that are stored there, and how, in a large
manuscript collection of harpsichord music dating from
the sixteenth century, he had extracted the noble theme
which he was to employ to such good purpose in his
opera as well as in the march written many years later
for the Coronation of King Edward vii.

"The musical library of Buckingham Palace," he
writes, "is extremely curious, and it is extremely regrettable that it is not easier of access. One sees there,
amongst others, the manuscripts of the oratorios of
Handel, mostly written with a disconcerting rapidity.
The *Messiah* was composed in fifteen days! The
rudimentary instrumentation of the period renders the
thing possible; but who would nowadays be able to
write all those fugal choruses with such celerity?"

Without in any way wishing to disparage the genius
of Handel, it is necessary to remember that when short
of ideas or if pressed for time he did not hesitate to turn
to account some former composition of his own. In

the *Messiah*, for instance, the theme of the famous chorus " For unto us a child is born " had already figured in one of the Saxon master's Italian duets. It is to be feared that Handel did not confine himself to quoting from his own works, as may be realized by a perusal of Sedley Taylor's interesting volume entitled *The Indebtedness of Handel to Works by Other Composers*, from which the above information is taken.

The composition of such an important work as *Henry VIII* pursued by Saint-Saëns while leading the same feverish existence as before, interrupted first by one thing, then by another, by concert tours, by the composition of a Hymn to Victor Hugo, etc., progressed slowly. In the meanwhile he had been elected a member of the Institute in the place of Henri Reber, recently deceased.

The first performance of *Henry VIII* took place, after many delays, on March 5, 1883, with every promise of success. Extenuated by the fatigues of continuous rehearsals spread over six months, Saint-Saëns yielded to the strenuous orders of his doctor to take a well-earned rest, and soon after the production of his opera he packed up his trunks and hurried away to recuperate in the genial climate of Algeria. A too speedy return necessitated a cure at Cauterets and a further period of rest. When at last he was back in Paris, at the beginning of October, he had the gratification of finding *Henry VIII* on the bills of the Opéra, and of hearing that a project was being considered of performing his *Étienne Marcel* at the Théâtre du Château d'Eau.

Having regained his health, Saint-Saëns soon found himself again plunged in a vortex of excitement. More work, more concerts, more successes! In the midst of

all this he was able, however, to concentrate his mind
upon the composition of a work of capital importance,
the Symphony in C minor, written expressly for the
London Philharmonic Society and performed for the
first time at one of the Society's concerts on May 19,
1886, under the composer's direction. The redoubtable
key of C minor served him well, in spite of unavoidable
associations, and the symphony in question not only
represents his greatest achievement in this *genre*, but
counts among the finest modern works of its kind. It is
dedicated " to the memory of Franz Liszt," this master's
death having occurred on July 31 of the same year,
and before the publication of the Symphony which
Saint-Saëns intended to dedicate to him.

After the production of this great Symphony, Saint-
Saëns again turned his attention to the operatic stage,
and the year 1887 witnessed the production at the
Opéra-Comique of a new " lyrical drama " from his pen
entitled *Proserpine*, which created a favourable impression
on the whole, the second act especially taking the fancy
of the audience.

Indefatigable as ever, the composer now set to work
on a five-act opera with Benvenuto Cellini as the centre
figure. In deference to the memory of Berlioz, who had
written an opera of that name, it was decided to call the
work *Ascanio*, and it was under this appellation that it
was produced for the first time at the Paris Grand Opéra
on March 31, 1890.

Saint-Saëns did not assist at the production of his
new opera. Anxious to escape from the agitations and
anxieties of a first performance, and to restore his health,
which had suffered owing to excess of work, he left
Paris and did not return for several months. In order

2

to enjoy perfect rest and to be free from worrying letters, he took another name and left no address. After some time his continued absence began to cause uneasiness, and endeavours were made to discover his retreat. Finally he was run to earth at Las Palmas in the Canary Islands, where he had been recruiting and leading the simple life amidst the luxuriant beauties and in the soothing atmosphere of the tropics. Musical composition had been entirely laid aside during these months of *dolce far niente*, of delightful excursions, of reading, of pleasant intercourse with chance companions ignorant of his identity. Once recognized and everything was changed. He now found himself surrounded by hosts of people who were anxious to pay him homage and who, with the best intentions, as he wrote himself, rendered his life insupportable.

It was probably during these months of calm that he wrote some of the poems and verses published in a little volume entitled *Rimes Familières*, a charming collection of thoughts clothed in polished language, expressive of many moods, now tender, now sad, now good-humoured, now grimly ironical, and ending with a so-called *Bouffonerie antique*, a species of duologue bearing the strange title of " Botriocéphale," the characters being a faun and a fury.

The love of travel and the desire to spend the winter months in a warm climate had become irresistible, and in December 1891 he started again, and this time went farther afield in pursuit of health and relaxation, pushing on as far as Ceylon, where he busied himself in making alterations to his opera *Proserpine*, a new version of which was given at the Opéra-Comique some years later, in 1899.

On his return journey to Europe he stopped in Egypt and settled for a time in Cairo, where he wrote the Fantasia for piano and orchestra entitled " Africa." After a short sojourn in France he migrated to Algeria, and while there found distraction in writing a comedy entitled *La Crampe des écrivains*, which was performed at the Municipal Theatre of Algiers.

Two works of different character occupied him about this time : the first, *Phryné*, an *opéra-comique* in two acts, which was produced with great success at the Opéra-Comique Theatre on March 24, 1893, and the other his second Trio, in E minor. Several other compositions of less importance were penned between whiles by this truly astonishing musician.

In the month of June 1893 he went to Cambridge to receive the honorary degree of Doctor of Music conferred upon him, as well as upon Max Bruch, Tchaikovsky, Boïto, and Grieg, all being present with the exception of the last-named.

Saint-Saëns has written a charming description of his stay in the famous University town, of the ceremony of investiture, the concert given in honour of the new Doctors of Music, the hospitality he received, etc. He was evidently delighted with his reception, and did not lose the opportunity of expressing his feelings. " Everything has been said concerning English hospitality," he wrote, " and really one could not say too much ; never obsequious, it surrounds one with attentions without embarrassing one or imposing any more or less tiresome duties ; and in these vast dwellings, supplied with every imaginable comfort, one has the feeling that one is not in the way."

The entire account of his Cambridge experiences is

written in a thoroughly pleasant and genial style. He
expresses a childish delight in the ceremony when " at
the head of the group of Doctors marched the King of
Bahonagar, his gold turban sparkling with fabulous
stones and a collar of diamonds round his neck," and
gives an interesting account of the concert at which he
played the solo part in his own Fantasia, " Africa."
He ends by saying that he has " returned confirmed,
once more, in the idea that the English love and understand music, and that a contrary opinion is a prejudice.
They love it in their own way, which is their right ;
but that way is not such a bad one, considering that
art owes to it the oratorios of Handel, the great symphonies of Haydn, Weber's opera *Oberon*, the *Elijah*, and
the Scottish Symphony of Mendelssohn, the *Redemp-
tion* and *Mors et Vita* of Gounod, all works written
for England, and which without her would probably
never have been born. I have always maintained this
thesis, from love of truth ; to this sentiment is now added
that of gratitude, which I am happy to have the opportunity of expressing."

A few months before the above-mentioned Cambridge
function, Saint-Saëns had appeared in London at a
memorable concert of the Philharmonic Society, when
he had shared the honours of the occasion with Tchaikovsky, whose sad death was to take place in the autumn
of the same year.

On this occasion Saint-Saëns played the solo part in
his popular Concerto in G minor and conducted his
Rouet d'Omphale, while Tchaikovsky conducted his
Symphony in F, No. 4, now so well known and justly
admired. A particularly interesting opportunity was
thus offered of contrasting the styles of two of the

most famous contemporary composers — the French master's music, exquisitely polished and refined, flowing on with unerring expressive facility and without a superfluous note ; that of the other, wilder and more passionate, either revelling in its anguish or else bursting forth in an unbridled exuberance of spirits. It is the fashion nowadays to consider Tchaikovsky as being more cosmopolitan than essentially Russian in his music. Whatever alien influences may be detected therein, it is certainly impossible to imagine any but a Russian being able to write works such as the Symphonies and the piano Concerto.

As the years followed one another, Saint-Saëns showed no signs of abating the feverish productivity which had characterized him from the earliest days of his career. Amidst his many labours he undertook the difficult task of completing the score of an opera entitled *Frédégonde*, left unfinished by his friend Ernest Guiraud, which was produced at the Paris Opéra on December 16, 1895.

He did not, however, allow this work to prevent him from indulging in his favourite love of travel, for, while he was engaged in setting to music the unfinished portions of the above opera, his wanderings took him to the Far East, where he visited Saïgon, the capital of Cochin-China, and other places.

In 1896 a Jubilee concert was given in Paris to celebrate the fiftieth anniversary of his first appearance in public.

A new outlet for his creative genius was now at hand. Some arenas were in course of construction at Béziers, in the south of France. These had been originally

destined for bull-fights. It occurred to M. Castelbon
de Beauxhostes, a wealthy musical amateur, that they
might be utilized for the purpose of open-air theatrical
performances with music. Saint-Saëns was much taken
with the idea, and his friend Louis Gallet having written
a tragedy on a classical subject entitled *Déjanire*, he
lost no time in composing an important score for this
work. The two performances, which took place in
August 1898, attracted enormous audiences. It is said
that quite ten thousand spectators were present, and
Saint-Saëns, who conducted, had an immense orchestral
force under his baton, besides a large male and female
chorus.

At the close of that year, the indefatigable traveller,
after a sojourn in his favourite Canary Islands, accepted
an invitation to visit the Argentine Republic, and pro-
ceeded to Buenos Ayres, where he gave concerts of
Chamber music.

The constant change of scene, climate, general conditions, language, etc., all seem to have stimulated his
vivid imagination and doubtless account for much of
the variety in his musical production. In this respect
he does not resemble the average Frenchman, whose
distaste of travel is notorious.

Having got rid of one work, he has generally found
relaxation by commencing another of a different kind.
Thus, after his triumphs at Béziers and his South
American successes, he wrote a String Quartet and
dedicated it to Ysaye, with whom he appeared at
concerts in Brussels. In May 1900, *Le Feu Céleste*, a
cantata from his pen in praise of electricity, was produced
at the first grand official concert given at the Paris
Exhibition.

A work of greater importance now occupied his mind, the composition of a lyrical drama originally intended to be performed in the arenas of the town of Orange, but subsequently altered and adapted to the stage of the Paris Opéra, where it was produced on October 23, 1901, the title being *Les Barbares* and the librettists Victorien Sardou and Gheusi. Although well received, this opera has not remained in the répertoire.

The following year, 1902, Saint-Saëns was occupied in writing music for a piece entitled *Parysatis*, played the August of that year in the arenas of Béziers. This same year he composed a Coronation March in honour of King Edward VII.

His next operatic venture took the form of a one-act "lyrical poem" entitled *Hélène*, of which he wrote words and music, and which was given for the first time at Monte Carlo in February 1905. That same year it was heard in London at Covent Garden, the part of the erring wife of Menelaus being enacted by Mme Melba.

Another opera, *L'Ancêtre*, was produced the February following, also at Monte Carlo.

In the autumn of 1906 Saint-Saëns visited the United States, but was taken seriously ill on the journey out. During the whole of his stay there he had to battle against ill-health, but he nevertheless refused to give in, and managed to appear at Philadelphia, Chicago, and Washington. After this trying time on the other side of the Atlantic, in recollection of which he set to music the psalm "Praise ye the Lord," he went to Cairo, where he wrote incidental music for Brieux's drama *La Foi*.

In 1907 he was present at the inauguration of his own

statue at Dieppe, the town which contains the exceptionally interesting museum bearing his name and includes every kind of memento of his career.

Déjanire, another opera on a large scale, now occupied him. This was an operatic version of Louis Gallet's tragedy of the same name, for which he had written music some years previously. In its new form *Déjanire* was heard for the first time at Monte Carlo on March 14, 1911, and was given at the Paris Opéra on November 22 in the same year. Like several of the composer's other operas *Déjanire* made a good start, but its success was not maintained.

Saint-Saëns was present in London on June 2, 1913, at a Jubilee Festival which took place at the Queen's Hall in his honour, and to celebrate the seventy-fifth anniversary of his musical career, that is calculating it from the time when he took his first lesson on the piano at the age of two and a half years. The programme of the concert was entirely devoted to works by the hero of the occasion, with the exception of a Concerto of Mozart, the solo part of which was played by the master himself. The principal item was the great Symphony in C minor, a singularly appropriate choice if only for the reason that its original production had taken place in London. An Album containing the signatures of the most prominent musical personalities of the London world was presented to the composer by Mr. Hermann Klein, and an Address on behalf of the general Committee was read by Sir Alexander Mackenzie. In the course of this Address the composer was thus apostrophied : "Amid the varied developments of modern music, you have worthily upheld the highest traditions of your national Art ; you have been the champion of its cause and carried its classic banner from triumph to triumph. With ' progress ' for your watchword and with unique versatility, you led the advance of French music in every branch, and you are justly acknowledged to-day to be its most gifted and most exalted representative." Nothing could be truer, or better expressed.

In the autumn of the same year Saint-Saëns returned to England for the production at the Gloucester Musical Festival of a new oratorio from his pen entitled *The Promised Land*.

The great World War did not put a stop to his varied activities. Since 1914 he has published quite a number of works of different sorts, including pieces for different instruments, songs, choruses, a second String Quartet (in G, Op. 153), a " Marche interalliée," Op. 155. These two last works belong to the year 1919. He expressed his patriotic opinions forcibly in a booklet entitled *Germanophilie*, published in 1916.

On October 9, 1920, he celebrated his eighty-fifth birthday. The years had evidently dealt lightly with the famous musician, for his many admirers might have read the account of a concert which took place at the Trocadero in Paris during that month when the veteran and ever youthful master moved an audience to enthusiasm in the dual capacity of composer and executant.

Since then he has followed the swallows to warmer climes, and the newspapers have recorded the great success he has obtained at a concert in Algiers.

CHAPTER II

THE ARTIST

SAINT-SAËNS the musician and Saint-Saëns the man are so intimately allied that it is impossible to dissociate one from the other. The following words from Mr. Francesco Berger's delightful volume of Reminiscences convey an excellent idea of his appearance: "He is a man of middle stature, square-set, with a finely chiselled nose, and a wonderful pair of alert, penetrating eyes. He has a remarkable speaking-voice, loud and very shrill, and he utters so rapidly that it is difficult to follow him—his words flash from him like sparks from an anvil."

Great simplicity, affability, and an entire absence of ostentation are some of the master's prominent characteristics. He is always perfectly natural. As a conversationalist he is unapproachable. Possessing an encyclopædic knowledge on most subjects, he is an irresistibly fascinating " causeur," his conversation being punctuated by sallies of wit.

The strong will, determination, and decided opinions which have enabled him to fight his way upwards through so many difficulties are also easy to discern. A certain impassivity in his attitude on the concert

M. SAINT-SAËNS, ABOUT 1890

platform has led some to think him cold, a remark which also has been applied to him as a composer, possibly on account of the strict adherence to form which characterizes his compositions in the main, even when their formality has little in common with that of the older masters. His versatility has caused some to think him inconsistent, but certainly this is not a suitable term to apply to one who has devoted himself so seriously to his art and who has shown that, if he has the power to instil good spirits into the minds of his hearers, he can also elevate their thoughts and touch their hearts.

With some people lucidity of thought, clear and concise reasoning, denote superficiality, while dullness and incomprehensibility are hailed as profundity. Voltaire has been termed superficial. In him and in Saint-Saëns may be noted that particular lucidity of expression and clear logical thought associated with their countrymen.

Saint-Saëns is as pre-eminently representative of the French race as Brahms is of the Teutonic. At the same time there is something of the cosmopolitan about him which does not exist in the latter. The following estimate of the French master written some years ago by Hanslick, the famous Viennese critic, the great friend and admirer of Brahms, is worth reading :

" Since Berlioz, Camille Saint-Saëns is the first musician who, not being a German, has written pure instrumental music, and created in that line, original and valuable works, the reputation of which have passed beyond the limits of France. Berlioz has exercised upon him an undoubted influence. To be convinced

of this it is only necessary to consider the titles of his
works, many of which belong to pictorial music, and
to observe certain effects of instrumentation after the
manner of Berlioz, such as the frequent use of harps,
the *pizzicati* of violins, etc. From these, however, it
should not be concluded that Saint-Saëns is an imitator
of Berlioz. . . . Despite his genius, Berlioz was lost
when he had no poetical matter to sustain him and
when he could not make use of colour. He was never
able to produce, like Saint-Saëns, a work exclusively
musical in form and idea, such as a Quintet or a Trio. . . .
Everywhere in the works of Saint-Saëns are found
spirit, humour, many qualities of scholarship, and
piquant vivacity of treatment. His compositions show
excellent workmanship and extreme facility in dealing
with all kinds of musical expression."

Some of the French master's critics have found it
difficult to discover a distinct personality in one whose
extraordinary versatility has enabled him to shine in
so many different styles of music, at one moment employing the scholastic forms of a past age and at another
displaying his familiarity with the most modern devices.
When Gounod paid him the doubtful compliment of
saying that " he could write at will a work in the style
of Rossini, of Verdi, of Schumann, or of Wagner," he
intended to draw attention to this very versatility,
and he took care to add that his knowledge of these
masters was a guarantee against his imitating any of
them.

Now perhaps the most dominant feature in the personality of Saint-Saëns is his absolute independence
of thought. His nature will brook no outside inter-

ference. This can be noted both in his music and in his writings. He hates what he terms *les enthousiasmes de commande*, and refuses to worship blindly at the shrine of the musical deity of the hour. Opposition acts upon him as a stimulant, and he is always ready to defend an unpopular cause with his pen.

To describe a musical personality so complex as his is no easy matter, and has puzzled more than one commentator. And yet this personality is so pronounced that it is discernible in nearly all his works. When Saint-Saëns alludes to Berlioz as a " musical paradox " he employs a term in reality far more applicable to himself. How indeed can one hope to convey an idea of a musical personality so consistent yet so wayward, so classical yet so romantic, so grave yet so gay ? How describe this protean composer who finds himself equally at home whether writing an opera, a string quartet, a symphony, or a simple song ?—this serious-minded musician who when seated at the organ can evoke the spirit of Bach, or in front of a piano can disclose the beauties of all the masters of the keyboard ?

Saint-Saëns is indeed absolutely unique and has no counterpart. He has found it possible to be learned without being pedantic, to be tuneful without becoming banal, to employ all musical forms with ease and absolute mastery of resource, to remain clear and concise in his musical utterances, and to avoid all exaggeration. His wide outlook on life has prevented him from ever falling into extremes one way or another, and has contributed to preserve that perfect equilibrium which exists in all his works. He has always remained absolutely master of himself, and the sound common sense engrafted in his nature has stood him in good stead in his life work.

The fact of his having employed so many forms associated with famous composers of the past has caused the originality of his music to be impugned. " One seems to be passing through scenery that one has seen formerly and that one loves," writes M. Romain Rolland, who hastens to add, " not that one can ever note direct resemblances ; nowhere perhaps are reminiscences rarer than with this master who carries in his memory all the ancient masters—-but it is by the spirit itself that he resembles them."

The fondness for placing in juxtaposition the musical phraseology of the past and that of the present shows itself repeatedly in the works of Saint-Saëns—in *Samson and Delilah*, for instance, the opening scene of which evokes the contrapuntal age of Bach and Handel, while the style of the music changes entirely with the appearance of the treacherous heroine.

All this, however, means nothing. The artistic personality of Saint-Saëns reveals itself in whatever style he chooses to adopt, and may be easily recognized. Every composer has a musical ancestry, and is more or less related to one, two, or more of his immediate predecessors. This does not in any way imply want of originality. Gounod has said that one might as well expect a son not to have a father as a composer not to have ancestors. Saint-Saëns has several, but if he reveres them he does not allow them to influence him unduly or to stem the flow of his own individual ideas. Beethoven's affinity with his two predecessors Haydn and Mozart is familiar enough, while Wagner owes something to quite a number of other composers, such as Weber, Meyerbeer, Mendelssohn, and Liszt. Yet this does not render the author of the famous nine Symphonies or the creator of *Tristan* any less great.

Saint-Saëns was nurtured from his earliest days on a solid classical musical diet. We have seen that he became familiar with the music of Mozart and Beethoven at an age when most children are still in the nursery. Later on, the serious trend of his mind showed itself when sixteen years old by the composition of a symphony, a form of music little cultivated in France at the time. Afterwards, in the organ-loft, he spent countless hours in company with the old Church composers of a bygone age, ranging backwards to the time of Gregory the Great. In the meanwhile his buoyant nature prevented him from developing into a dull, pedantic pundit.

A corrective against undue solemnity and pedantry was afforded him in his early home life. The weekly reunions which took place at one time in the apartment he occupied with his mother have not been forgotten. Monday evenings were devoted to these, and many of the most famous artists of the day gladly availed themselves of the invitation to attend them. Music naturally formed the great attraction of these evenings, with Saint-Saëns as *deus ex machina*. At times a spirit of fun was given free play, and it is said that on one occasion the gay young artists and their host attempted to perform Offenbach's *La Belle Hélène* in costume ! The worthy curé of the Madeleine might possibly have been surprised to see his organist thus occupied, though it is probable that he would have been much amused. Saint-Saëns went so far as to compose for the above reunions a one-act *opéra bouffe* entitled *Gabriella di Vergy* as a parody of the old Italian opera style. In 1885 this piece was performed at one of the soirées of the Society known as La Trompette. It was thus described : " *Pochade mi-carême carnavalesque, en parodie d'un opéra Italien, composée (paroles et musique) par un ancien organiste (œuvre de jeunesse).*" It is said that on one occasion, in the salon of Mme Viardot, Saint-Saëns took part in a charade in which he appeared, in costume, as Marguerite in the Jewel scene from *Faust* !

The gay, sunny nature of the composer, his love of fun and sense of humour can be realized by the above.

In his younger days his leisure hours were employed in a manner calculated to prevent any cobwebs from accumulating. He has related himself that he never lost an opportunity of visiting the Opéra-Comique, and how he used to enjoy the light operas of Auber, which then formed the chief musical pabulum offered to the habitués of this theatre.

Many years later, the typically national *opéra-comique* of the past, now somewhat out of favour, found a perhaps unexpected defender in one whose artistic ideas seemed to point in another direction, albeit he had not disdained to make a passing excursion that way. At any rate Saint-Saëns attempted the defence of the *genre* in a witty article which began in the following promising manner : " A curious book might be written on *intolerance in the matter of art.*" The italics are his own. " This malady," he continues, " which our epoch has not invented, rages at present over the amiable *genre* of the *opéra-comique* : it becomes urgent to look into the matter, and I venture to do so at the risk of hearing more remarks about my versatility, comparable to that which consists in getting up in the morning and going to bed in the evening, clothing myself lightly in summer, warmly in winter, all things about which no one thinks of being scandalized."

He then proceeds to relate how fond he was in his youth of the old *opéra-comique*, in spite of the worship he bestowed on the fugues of Sebastian Bach and the symphonies of Beethoven, and breaks a lance in favour of the old style of *opéra-comique* with spoken dialogue, pointing out its advantage in the case of the adaptation to the lyrical stage of " amusing and complicated comedies, the plot of which could not be developed without many words, incomprehensible if these words did not reach the ears of the public without obstacle."

Whether this reasoning will prove convincing to the devotees of modern opera is doubtful, but it is interesting as emanating from such an authority. Formerly, when operas consisted of detachable pieces, it was the custom to employ either recitatives or spoken dialogue as connecting links. Nowadays the general habit as regard works of serious import is to adopt the Wagnerian plan of making the music follow the action of the piece without break. Let us not forget, though, as Saint-Saëns points out, that Weber's *Der Freischütz* and Beethoven's *Fidelio* belong to the much-abused *genre*, inasmuch as singing in these works " alternates with dialogue," and that if this has been set to music by others, who can tell whether either Weber or Beethoven would have approved of the transformation ? He might also have added that both Gounod's *Faust* and Bizet's *Carmen* originally contained spoken dialogue. Still, it is generally accepted nowadays that the music should be continuous in operas that are seriously conceived, whether the subject treated be of a tragic order or partake of the nature of comedy.

3

The apparent inconsistency and lack of fixed purpose in his ideas of operatic forms having met with repeated criticism, Saint-Saëns had felt impelled to deal with the matter definitely in a letter which he wrote to the editor of the *Carillon Théâtral* soon after the production of his opera *Proserpine* (1887). After saying that each time he produces a new work on the stage and whenever he deviates from " the symphonic and declamatory form " he is accused of pandering to the popular taste or of being false to his " most cherished theories and principles," he proceeds thus : " My theory of dramatic art is this : I believe that the drama is progressing towards a synthesis of different elements, song, declamation, and symphony blending in an equilibrium which I seek, and which others will one day find. Both heart and head impel me to pursue this aim, and to this I must adhere. . It is for this reason that I am disowned now by those Wagnerians who despise the melodic style and the art of singing, now by those reactionaries who lay the entire stress on these elements, and consider other elements mere accessories."

It must be remembered that the above words, which certainly denote a very sensible and logical way of thinking, were written in 1887, at a time when Wagner's theories were still being ardently discussed. Many years have passed since then, and many attempts have been made, with more or less success, to blend the various elements above mentioned. " All composers," he wrote, " are seeking new methods," and he considered that these were " in the direction of the synthesis, the equilibrium which will be the last word of Dramatic Act, if Art can have a last word."

Saint-Saëns was right to guard himself with this

last sentence. He could not foretell that a further evolution in operatic art might lead not to the synthesis of the elements he mentions, but to their absolute disappearance, and that a composer would arise who would write an opera in which song, declamation, and symphony would be totally absent ; that in the place of song and declamation there would be substituted a species of vocal speech which bore little resemblance to either, while an undercurrent of shifting harmonies in the orchestra would take the place of symphonic development ; in other words, he could not anticipate Debussy and his *Pelléas et Mélisande* ! What the future development of operatic form may lead to, it is impossible to say. Whether this form of art will disappear entirely and vanish in atmospherical attempts to outdo Debussy, or survive in frenetic endeavours to emulate and surpass the complicated scores of Richard Strauss, *chi lo sa* ! Is it possible that the dancer, or *mime*, will eventually supplant the vocalist ? I cannot think so. " Pelléas " is an exception. Debussy had a very individual style of his own. To imitate him is to court disaster. His influence might easily have a debilitating effect on those who attempt to follow him too closely. Happily there are now French composers who have not done so, but have struck out paths of their own, Alfred Bruneau, Charpentier, Henri Rabaud, amongst others.

One thing certain, as far as it is possible to tell, is that the public is not likely for a long while to abandon the cult of what is understood as melody, and that an opera which contains nothing which can by any stretch of the imagination pass for this is highly unlikely to become really popular in any sense of the word. Formerly the love of melody, or one might say of tune, was so powerful that the presence of this element covered a multitude of sins or shortcomings. These were the early days of the nineteenth century when Italian composers turned out an opera in a few weeks.

As time went on and musical taste improved, the public became more difficult. This is not intended as a disparagement of composers such as Rossini, Bellini, and Donizetti, whose beautiful melodies delighted their generation and the next. Rossini when he wrote *William Tell* (1829) for the Paris Opéra enlarged his style, and Donizetti did the same some years later in *La Favorite* (1840).

The production of Meyerbeer's *Robert le Diable* (1831) and especially of *Les Huguenots* (1836) raised the opera to hitherto undreamed-of heights. These two works, while abounding in melodies, contained new elements of abiding worth, picturesque details, characterization of the dramatis personæ, vivid orchestral colouring. They prepared the way for the operas of Wagner, Verdi, Gounod, and many others. Yet there are musicians who lose no opportunity of speaking slightingly of their composer! Saint-Saëns is not one of these. His opinion of Meyerbeer has been expressed in an article, allusion to which will be found in the last chapter of the present volume.

It will be realized that there is nothing mean or narrow in the ideas of Saint-Saëns concerning music generally. He is ready to admire and enjoy works of entirely different styles, provided these appear to him good of their kind. His hatred of intolerance in the matter of art equals that of Voltaire when he wrote his plea in favour of tolerance and said : " We are all of us made up of weakness and errors ; let us reciprocally forgive each other our follies, this is the first law of nature."

Certainly Voltaire was pleading in favour of religious tolerance, which is not quite the same thing. Yet it is not so different as might be imagined. To the enthusiastic musician his art is as sacred as a religion. It breeds fanaticism just as readily: the many quarrels between the partisans of opposite schools of musical thought and the intolerance displayed on either side prove this. On the other hand, it may be contended that the fervent believer, whether in art or religion, will necessarily become intolerant of other ways of thinking for the reason that being so thoroughly convinced of the truth of his own special belief he naturally looks upon all others as wrong, and if, in some instances, he contents himself with becoming an apostle preaching the good news to all and sundry, in others he degenerates into a persecutor. The melancholy history of the wars of religion affords but too ample a proof of this. Now the different partisans of hostile musical camps have never had the power to impose their own views with the aid of the stake or the axe, but they have often added greatly to the difficulties experienced by musicians with a new message to deliver, and this on account of that very intolerance in the matter of art to which Saint-Saëns objects.

In this connection it must not be inferred that tolerance in art implies weakness or the lack of any definite ideals. Neither does it prevent a musician from having his own preferences, but it prevents him from doing what is so often done: condemning wholesale on insufficient grounds and perhaps even without a cursory knowledge of the work or the composer.

To hold large views on artistic matters implies the possession of a superior intellect, one which is able to discriminate between the true artist and the quack. Liszt possessed such an intellect, and we know what an enormous amount he was able to achieve and how admirably he used his influence to further the progress of his art. The opinions of Saint-Saëns on music and musicians, as well as on other subjects, will be alluded to in a later chapter dealing with his writings. Enough has been said here to convey an idea of the comprehensiveness of his musical outlook, which may to a certain extent explain how he has been led to adopt so many different forms and styles for the expression of his thoughts.

In England, Saint-Saëns is better known in the concert-room than in connection with opera, notwithstanding the great and abiding success of *Samson and Delilah*, which made so tardy an appearance on the London operatic boards. The only two other operas of his that have been heard here, *Henry VIII* and *Hélène*, have not been played sufficiently often to make a lasting impression.

It is different as regards his instrumental works. Many of these have long since occupied permanent places in our concert programmes, and may be said to count as classics. The Symphonic Poems, *Le Rouet d'Omphale*, *Phaeton*, *Danse Macabre*, the second and fourth piano Concertos, the third violin Concerto, to name a few of his best known and most typical compositions, are constantly heard and greatly appreciated. The same remark applies to his Chamber music, trios, quartet, sonatas, etc. It is through these works that he is best known in England, and they are sufficient to enable one to form an estimate of his style and individuality.

In the matter of technique Saint-Saëns has been universally recognized as a past master. There is here no divergence of opinion. "The most individual feature of his moral physiognomy seems to me to be a melancholy languor." So writes M. Romain Rolland, adding that this "has its source in a rather bitter sentiment of the nothingness of things, with fits of lassitude of a somewhat sickly nature, succeeded by fits of a somewhat fantastic humour, of nervous gaiety, of a capricious taste for parody, burlesque, the comical."

The "melancholy languor" alluded to by the eminent writer is perhaps expressed in certain poems, included in the *Rimes Familières*, but there is not much trace of it in the composer's music. On the contrary, if there exists one whose music might in general be considered expressive of optimism it is surely that of Saint-Saëns.

The joy of life often pulsates in its rhythmical accents. When his music is sad or of a contemplative nature, it never tears unduly at one's heart's strings or probes too far into the depths of grief. Indeed, it often acts as a veritable tonic to jaded nerves, like a bottle of sparkling wine. This is a point that deserves to be noted. Music should be a benefit to mankind. It should comfort those who are in trouble and give them courage to fight against adversity. Some composers, instead of trying to do this, appear to take a pleasure in accentuating grief or in irritating the nerves, and leave their unfortunate hearers more miserable than ever. This cannot as a rule be said of Saint-Saëns, and, if for this reason only, he deserves well of humanity.

At the beginning of his career his familiarity with classical forms had the effect of alarming some people and procuring for him the reputation of being aridly scientific and lacking melody. It is really amusing to note the various and totally opposite opinions called forth by his music. At one time he was accused of being too much influenced by Wagner, at another of not being sufficiently so.

As regards the accusation of being too scientific, he replied to it in the following airy manner : " A musician is asked to hide his science. Now, what is meant by science in this case is simply talent, and when one has got any it is to use and not to put into one's pocket." He has also made short work of the reproach that he has changed his mind with regard to Wagner, by whom as a matter of fact he has never been much influenced, unless it be through the employment of representative themes in some of his operas : even then, his methods and those of the German master have not much in common.

On the other hand, he owes something to Berlioz and more to Liszt and Gounod. The first of these, in his great Treatise on Instrumentation, discoursed on the possibilities of the modern orchestra in language often poetical if sometimes extravagant. Saint-Saëns says that it is through this work that all the musicians of his generation were formed. It had " the inestimable quality of inflaming the imagination, of making one love the art it taught. What it did not teach, it gave one the desire to learn, and one only knows thoroughly that which one has learnt oneself."

Liszt, by his priceless creation of the Symphonic Poem, disclosed new vistas of art and opened the road

along which many composers, and Saint-Saëns one of
the first, were destined to travel. The influence of
Gounod is of a more special nature and asserts itself
occasionally in the contour of certain melodies and
through the employment of harmonies associated with
the composer of *Faust*, whose influence may be said
to have been paramount in France for several years
after the production of this opera. A slight Mendels-
sohnian influence may be detected in some of the earlier
instrumental compositions of Saint-Saëns, but this is
of a very superficial nature. Bach also, as we have
seen, has had something to do with giving the composer
that solidity and firmness he has so often displayed.

Saint-Saëns, endowed with so impressionable a nature,
quite naturally has fallen under the charm of the
Southern and Eastern climes where he has so often
sought rest from his arduous labours. This accounts
for the presence in some of his works of certain characteristic elements associated with Oriental and other exotic
music.

In his choice of subjects for musical illustration he
has also shown his great versatility of taste. Classical,
Biblical, and mythological subjects have inspired him to
write some of his best works, notably the spinning-wheel
of Omphale, the ill-fated attempt of Phaeton to drive
the chariot of the Sun, the youth of Hercules; and in
his operas, the story of Samson and Delilah, that of
Helen of Troy, and again, that of the courtesan Phryne.
The fantastic and the weird have also fascinated him,
as we know by the *Danse Macabre*, so universally and
justly popular. He has delved into history and brought
to the mind visions of past centuries. His own essentially
modern personality, which is not exempt from a certain

ironical sense of humour, has never lost itself in its wanderings through the different realms of sound.

Gounod once summed him up in the following words : " Saint-Saëns possesses one of the most astonishing musical organizations that I know. He is a musician armed with every weapon. He possesses his art like no one else; he knows the masters by heart; he plays with and makes light of the orchestra as he plays with and makes light of the piano, which says everything. He is neither finicking, nor violent, nor emphatic. He has no system, he belongs to no party, to no clique; he does not pose as a reformer of anything; he writes as he feels and with what he knows."

CHAPTER III

OPERAS

SAINT-SAËNS had to wait a long time and to contend against many difficulties before he was able to make his début as a composer of operas. He relates himself that he was wont to say to his friend and colleague Georges Bizet, " As they do not want us in the theatre, let us take refuge in the concert-room," to which the future composer of *Carmen* used to reply, " You speak at your ease, I am not made for the Symphony ; I must have the theatre without which I can do nothing." Saint-Saëns adds, " He was evidently mistaken ; a musician of his worth is everywhere in his place."

Whether this is the case, however, is open to doubt, as all composers do not possess the versatility of a Saint-Saëns. Some are pre-eminently fitted to shine as composers of opera, whereas others show little aptitude in this direction. Schumann, for example, in *Genoveva*, his only opera, proved that his introspective genius was ill at ease amid stage surroundings. Yet he was certainly not devoid of dramatic power, as may be seen by his magnificent setting of the Church scene in *Faust*.

Curiously enough, in the same article from which the

above words are taken, Saint-Saëns explains the difference
in the point of view which then existed between Bizet
and himself, and as this bears to a certain extent on the
question, it may as well be quoted. After praising his
friend's loyalty and sincerity, features common to both
their characters, he states that in other ways they differed
entirely, " each one pursuing a different ideal : he,
seeking before all passion and life ; I, running after the
chimera of purity of style and perfection of form. Thus
our conversations never ended ; our friendly discussions
had a vivacity and a charm that I have found with no
one since."

Purity of style and perfection of form—these are
indeed qualities which characterize the music of Saint-
Saëns to a supreme degree. They are inherent in his
nature and are present in all his compositions whether
for the concert-room or the theatre. In the works he
has written for the stage they have not prevented him
from depicting with success scenes of passion and life,
but have enabled him to keep an absolute control over
his means of expression and to bend these to his will.
In other words, his feeling for purity of style and perfection of form has guarded him against anything approaching blatant vulgarity on the one hand and incoherent ravings on the other. His muse has always
been tastefully and decently clothed on the stage and
elsewhere. " His lyrical dramas," observes M. Emile
Baumann, " harmonious point of junction between
the past and the future, are more than any others a
faithful expression of the French ideal, the union of
the pathetic with reason, of noble song and moving
psychology, of instrumental power and scenic animation."

LA PRINCESSE JAUNE

Opéra-Comique in one Act. Words by Louis Gallet.
Produced at the Opéra-Comique Theatre, Paris, June 12,
1872.

Although he had an operatic work of larger dimensions
in readiness, it was by a modest one-act piece that Saint-
Saëns made his operatic début. It cannot be said that
the result was a particularly encouraging one, the piece
only attaining five performances, six less than had been
accorded to Bizet's *Djamileh*, produced at the same theatre
a few weeks previously. Both works were blamed by
certain critics on the score of incoherency and bizarre
harmonies, a blame which seems incomprehensible to-day.
Félix Clément, in his *Dictionary of Operas*, gravely
admonished the composer of the *Princesse Jaune* for
his desire to avoid the usual paths of music, and told
him that in so doing he had greatly compromised his
reputation. As this same Clément was unable to discover any beauty in the Prelude to *Lohengrin*, the value
of his opinion scarcely counts, except that it affords an
instance of the antagonism towards any new departure
in music which was not uncommon among certain musical
writers in Paris at that time.

Paladilhe, another composer whose first operatic
venture, *Le Passant*, also a one-act piece, had been
produced earlier in the year at the same theatre, had
incurred the same sort of reproach. He was accused
by one critic of belonging to what he was pleased to
term " the school of the musical labyrinth." Anyone
who knows the music of Paladilhe will realize how little
such a description could apply to it.

Bizet's charming *Djamileh* fared no better, one critic

saying that the composer, " wishing to astonish the public rather than pass unnoticed, was posing as an innovator endeavouring in his feverish dreams to snatch a few rays from the crown of the prophet Richard Wagner ! "

There is no doubt that at that time many representatives of musical opinion in Paris were obsessed by a continual fear of Wagner and his supposed influence. This moved Saint-Saëns to allude to the subject in a letter in which he said that it would be perhaps well to ask the critics who profess to hate Wagner why they should always be speaking of him on every possible occasion: "if a musician composes serious music, it is Wagner ; if another writes light music, capital, it is not Wagner ; if a locomotive whistles, again Wagner. It is stupid and annoying."

La Princesse Jaune certainly contained nothing calculated to alarm those suffering from Wagnerphobia, unless they went so far as to find a connection with *Tristan* in the fact that the plot dealt with the absorption of a narcotic drink ! But then they might as well have gone further back to the subjects of Auber's *Le Philtre* and Donizetti's *L'Elisire d'Amore* ! All this is futile.

The story related in verse by Louis Gallet hinges on the fancied infatuation for a Japanese statuette of a young Dutch scientist who, under the influence of a narcotic, fancies himself transported to Japan, and on awaking finds that his cousin who loves him is by his side.

This slight plot furnished Saint-Saëns with the opportunity of writing a dainty little score, without undue pretension, well suited to its theme, and prefixed by a delightfully quaint overture classical in form and exotic in colour.

This charming little curtain-raiser has been revived since at the Opéra-Comique.

LE TIMBRE D'ARGENT

Lyrical Drama in four Acts. Words by MICHEL CARRÉ
and JULES BARBIER. Produced at the Théâtre National
Lyrique, February 23, 1877.

Several years passed before Saint-Saëns produced a
successor to the above-mentioned little piece. The
story of *Le Timbre d'Argent*, which had been so to speak
" on the stocks " for some twelve years, bears a slight
resemblance to that of *La Princesse Jaune*, inasmuch
as the plot is equally unreal and turns out at the end
to have been but a dream. For this reason, an unfavour-
ably disposed critic called it " a nightmare in four acts
which lasts five hours." This seemingly ill-natured
remark is, however, not inappropriate as a description
of the story, which bears a certain resemblance to that
of *Faust*.

The evil one in this instance appears in the guise of
a certain Doctor Spiridion, who offers Conrad, a young
painter, eager to obtain gold in order to win the
graces of a dancer named Fiametta, a magic call-bell
which will gratify his desire each time he strikes it,
but at the same moment will cause the death of some-
one near him. Conrad accepts the offer and puts his
power to the test. A friend of his is immediately
struck down, but the sight of the gold quiets Conrad's
conscience. He now lives a sumptuous life of pleasure,
allured by the attractions of Fiametta, who always
eludes him, while at times his thoughts return to Hélène,
his betrothed. The climax arrives when, Fiametta
still being unapproachable, he strikes the magic call-
bell and his friend Benedict falls dead. The horror
of this wakens a chord in his heart. After hesitating

whether to follow the advice of Hélène or of Spiridion, he finally breaks the call-bell and—awakens to find that it has all been a dream !

This fantastic tale, owing to its unreality, was not of a nature calculated to produce a deep impression. It was another version dealing with the conflict between good and evil already operatically treated in *Robert le Diable*, *Tannhäuser*, and *Faust*. In this instance, however, the whole action of the piece turning out to be imaginary prevents the emotions of the characters from making any real appeal.

When we go to the opera we leave our common sense in the cloak-room with our overcoats, and enter prepared to accept all manner of impossibilities and incongruities if these are presented as realities and not as dreams or nightmares.

The supernatural figures in many famous operas and has proved a potent element of attraction, whether in *Don Giovanni*, *Freischütz*, *Robert le Diable*, *Faust*, *Tannhäuser*, with its curious mixture of Paganism and Christianity, and in all the other great Wagnerian music dramas with the exception of *Meistersinger*. But all these works, however impossible their stories, are presented as operatic versions of actual events and not as mere dreams. This is perhaps rather a far-fetched objection, but to the present writer it seems an important one. Anyhow, the probability is that the insuccess which attended *Le Timbre d'Argent* was more due to the librettists than to the composer.

The music written by Saint-Saëns to this unsatisfactory libretto is notable for its youthful exuberance. It has many of the qualities and also some of the defects of youth. Unequal as a whole, and denoting various

contradictory influences, it is by no means devoid of
charm, and if in parts it is somewhat suggestive of
Gounod, in others it bears the unmistakable imprint
of the composer's individuality.

Special mention must be made of the overture, which
seems somehow or other to have escaped the attention
of concert-givers in England. This is an extremely
brilliant piece, full of nervous energy, written with all
the composer's usual mastery, and which would surely
be welcomed if it were played occasionally in the place
of some of the hackneyed overtures with which we are
all so familiar.

The opera is interesting in many of its details, remarkable for excellence of workmanship, and contains several
attractive vocal numbers. It received a mixed reception
on the part of the critics. One considered it Wagnerian
in style, while another thought the contrary. One
praised its melodies, while another complained of their
absence, and so on. The opera did not remain long on
the bills, but was performed in Brussels some two years
later. In 1907 it was played at Monte Carlo and
has been given since elsewhere. It is interesting to
note that the arrangement of the vocal piano score
bears the name of Georges Bizet.

SAMSON ET DALILA

Opera in three Acts. Words by FERDINAND LEMAIRE.
German translation by RICHARD POHL. Produced at the
Grand Ducal Theatre of Weimar, December 2, 1877.

The composition of this work, which is universally
recognized as the composer's operatic masterpiece,
followed that of *Le Timbre d'Argent*, but it reveals
4

the genius of Saint-Saëns in an entirely different light. Handicapped somewhat in the former instance by an unsatisfactory libretto, he found here a theme worthy of his pen, simple and straightforward, and offering opportunities for great variety of treatment.

It may be mentioned that Saint-Saëns had composed the second act of this work before 1870, and that this was tried over privately, the part of Samson being sung by the unfortunate painter Henri Regnault, destined to lose his life on the battle-field not long after.

Doubtless discouraged by the scant prospects of ever having a work of this sort produced on the stage, Saint-Saëns had laid his score aside, when he was induced to take it up again by Liszt, who promised that he would have it performed at Weimar as soon as it was ready. The Franco-German War of 1870 delayed the fulfilment of this promise, which, however, was redeemed a few years later when the opera began its slow but triumphal progress and was gradually incorporated into the répertoires of the leading opera houses of the world. Only recently (August 1920) it has penetrated as far as California, where its success has been as great as elsewhere.

The symbolical nature of the Biblical story, exemplifying the triumph of weakness over strength, as well as its vividly human interest and profound psychological significance, were elements particularly calculated to appeal to the imagination of Saint-Saëns. In addition, there was here an opportunity of imparting touches of that Eastern colouring so dear to the composer. The result has been a work which not only counts among the composer's best, but ranks among the finest operas produced during the last fifty years.

No form of musical art suffers more from the hand of time than that known by the term opera. Reposing as it does purely on a convention, which changes in character almost with every generation, it is apt to show signs of age very rapidly whatever the quality of the music. In passing an opinion on any work, however good, written for the operatic stage, it is always necessary to bear this in mind. The intrinsic value of the music itself and its suitability to the text are often sufficient in themselves to ensure the vitality of an opera possessing superficial characteristics associated with the epoch in which it was written. This test may be applied to the most famous operas of the past.

When *Samson and Delilah* was first produced, it was considered by some to be musically in advance of its time. Discarding the old habit of cutting up an opera into detached pieces labelled song, duet, trio, chorus, etc., the composer had adopted the more modern plan of dividing his acts into scenes, then an unusual proceeding. A sparing but very telling use of recurring themes imparts consistency to a work composed of the most varied elements, one which contains scholastic devices suggestive of the old oratorios as well as sensuous melodies and luscious Eastern dances, and in which the composer has shown himself not only learned, but powerful, touching, and graceful in turns.

There is no overture. The work begins gravely and solemnly in the minor key, a fine effect being produced by the voices, first heard from behind the curtain, of the captive Israelites bewailing their lot. It has been remarked with truth that the opening scene is more suggestive of the oratorio than the opera. The Israelites express their feelings contrapuntally and possibly in

rather formal a manner. Musically this scene is admirably treated, though perhaps it is more effective in the
concert-room than on the stage. The arrival of Samson
brings greater animation and the music becomes more
and more dramatic. His rousing appeal stirs up the
drooping spirits of the captives. The entrance of the
satrap Abimelech puts a momentary stop to his eloquence.
In a quaint solo Abimelech taunts the Israelites, but
soon has cause to repent of his rashness, and falls an easy
victim to the anger of the crowd. The spirits of the
captives now being thoroughly aroused, headed by
Samson, they break their bonds and, after vigorously
shouting their theme of revolt, rush off the stage. Their
exit is succeeded by the appearance of the high priest
of Dagon, who gives vent to his fury in a forcible
monologue.

The stage being once more clear, the older Hebrews
enter and sing a rather monotonous psalm in celebration
of their deliverance. One is not sorry to see them go
and to welcome the appearance of Delilah. From now
onwards the music changes entirely in spirit, and the
remainder of the first act is a sheer enchantment for the
ear as well as for the eye.

The gates of the temple of Dagon having been thrown
open, Delilah enters, followed by Philistine girls, bearing
garlands of flowers in their hands, who celebrate the
victory of the Hebrews in strains of the most irresistible
charm. The temptress then addresses Samson in tender
and alluring accents, endeavouring to cast a spell over
him, while an old Hebrew utters words of warning.
In a languorous phrase of enveloping fascination she
begins to assert her conquest over Samson, who remains
deaf to the exhortations of the old Hebrew. The

priestesses of Dagon then come forward and endeavour to attract the Hebrew warriors by an enticingly
voluptuous dance, the music of which, mysteriously
subdued, is most original and taking. The act ends with
a song of penetrating charm in which Delilah sings of
the Spring, completes her victory over Samson and,
incidentally, of her audience.

The second act is laid in the valley of Sorek at nightfall,
outside the house of Delilah. Flashes of lightning
occasionally deck the sky. Delilah awaits Samson.
Her apostrophe to Love, if somewhat conventional in
form, is broadly melodious and extremely effective.
Fragments of this song reoccur subsequently. The high
priest of Dagon now comes to seek her aid against Samson,
and the two in a highly dramatic scene arrange to compass
his downfall. Then follows the great seduction scene,
concerning the beauty of which too much cannot be said.

Samson, though still hesitating, has been unable
entirely to resist the fascination of the enchantress.
He arrives, making feeble efforts to fight against the
spell she has cast over him. Her feigned passion is
expressed in strains of the most ardent nature. Still he
remains doubtful, until she changes her attitude, calls
him a coward, and disappears into her house. A momentary hesitation, and he hastens after her. Philistine
soldiers are now seen creeping slowly on to the stage
and gradually surrounding the house. Shortly afterwards, a cry of triumph from Delilah announces the
success of her treachery. Samson is lost.

To attempt to describe the musical beauties of the
above scene it would be necessary to indulge in many
superlatives. The entrancing nature of the melodies,
the vivid dramatic force, the contrasts between the

voluptuous accents of Delilah and Samson's vacillating appeals for strength to resist them, combine to render this one of the most remarkable scenes in the entire range of opera. It includes the well-known melody " Mon cœur s'ouvre à ta voix," which has contributed so much to popularize the opera and has been sung by so many vocalists, good, bad, and indifferent.

The third act is divided into two tableaux. The first of these represents the interior of the prison of Gaza, where Samson, blind and having lost his hair, is turning a hand-mill. In tones of the deepest anguish he appeals to Heaven for mercy. The poignant character of the situation is intensified by the voices of the Hebrews heard from behind the stage reproaching Samson for having abandoned them. This scene has been admirably treated by the composer, who has succeeded in realizing all its pathos without having recourse to complicated methods of expression.

The second tableau takes place in the interior of the temple of Dagon, whose statue occupies a prominent place therein. Samson has been brought in, and is now scoffed at by his enemies, while Delilah with a horrible refinement of cruelty reminds him of her past caresses, singing snatches of the melodies heard during the second act. The ballet, which precedes this, is delightful throughout and appropriately Eastern in style. The orgiac hymn to Dagon, treated in canon, is highly original and inspiriting. Its climax is interrupted by the voice of Samson, who, placed between two pillars, implores Heaven to give him back his strength if only for a moment. His prayer is granted, he seizes hold of the pillars, the temple subsides burying all who are within, and the opera comes to an abrupt close.

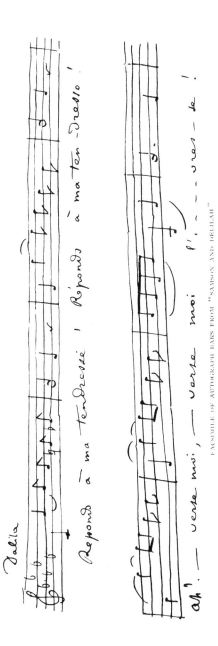

FACSIMILE OF AUTOGRAPH BARS FROM "SAMSON AND DELILAH"

The dual nature of the composer's genius is exemplified
to perfection in this opera by the employment of classical
as well as romantic elements, notable in affording the
contrasts between the lamentations of the captive
Hebrews and the truculent revelries of the Philistines.
A strict interpretation of the text, vivid characterization, strong contrasts, brilliant instrumental colouring, a
discreet use of leading themes, a steady flow of melodious
ideas, a distinct individuality of style in spite of certain
passing influences—these points are all realized in *Samson
and Delilah*, concerning which it may be said that the
composer has achieved unity in variety.

ÉTIENNE MARCEL

Opera in four Acts. Words by Louis Gallet. Produced
at Lyons, February 8, 1879.

This opera is different in character to the Biblical
work discussed above, and has certain points in common
with the grand operas of Meyerbeer and Halévy. For
this the subject is mainly responsible. Saint-Saëns
had the idea at the time of setting to music certain
episodes of the history of France, and the present work
was the first outcome of this intention. It was destined
also to be the last.

The action takes place in the year 1358 and the scene
is laid in Paris under the regency of the Dauphin Charles,
during the captivity in England of King John the
Good.

The subject is by no means a bad one, dealing as
it does with scenes of popular ferment, with Étienne
Marcel, the provost of the merchants, as its central
figure. Students of history need not be told that the
protagonist of the piece headed the revolt of the Parisian

people against the Dauphin Charles, that owing to the
fickleness of the mob, justified in those troublous times,
he lost his popularity and agreed to open the gates
of Paris to the troops of Charles the Bad, King of
Navarre. This act of treachery he paid for with his
life, and was assassinated by the demagogue Maillart.
The love element naturally is not absent in the opera,
and is furnished by Beatrice, daughter of Étienne
Marcel, and Robert de Lorris, equerry to the Dauphin.
Its course, according to precedent, does not run smooth.
After Marcel has been killed, his daughter throws herself
on his body while her lover endeavours to induce her
to follow him. The Dauphin enters with a flourish of
trumpets and the opera ends amid general rejoicing.

The four acts of the opera take place amid much
popular effervescence, and abound in dramatic situations,
while the opportunities for spectacular display are such
that the work is one eminently suited for performance
at the Paris Grand Opéra, where curiously enough it
has never been played. It was given some years ago
in Paris, not under the best conditions, during the
course of a season of opera at the Théâtre du Château
d'Eau.

The work certainly merited a better fate and should
not be allowed to fall into oblivion, for the music written
by Saint-Saëns contains much that is excellent, and
the opera is extremely interesting as a whole. The
charming ballet music, however, has survived, and is
occasionally heard in the concert-room. It consists
of six numbers and includes a *Musette militaire* and a
Pavane appropriately archaic in style. The presence
of a waltz in a work the action of which is laid in the
Middle Ages is somewhat disconcerting. Anachronisms

of this kind have, however, been frequent in opera. Gounod, for instance, did not scruple to introduce a waltz into the ballet of his opera *The Queen of Sheba*, and another into the additional music he wrote for the Brocken scene in the fifth act of *Faust*. He went even to further lengths, for in his *Polyeucte*, an opera laid in the early Christian times, he not only introduced a waltz but a mazurka as well. After all, did not the impeccable Gluck show equal unconcern for historical accuracy by introducing Gavottes, Minuets, and Chaconnes into his operas?

In *Étienne Marcel* Saint-Saëns has characterized the physiognomy of the Parisian crowd with peculiar felicity. The scenes of riot and violence are treated with power and at the same time with perfect lucidity, while the brighter portions are depicted with a light touch.

Nothing more delightfully ironical exists than the song " Le bon sénéchal de Poitiers," sung in the first act by a braggart concerning one of his intrigues. The sun shines in much of the music of *Étienne Marcel*, and when the clouds appear they are never too opaque. There is great tenderness expressed in certain cantilenas, such as the touching complaint of the Dauphin, " Parfois je songe en ma tristesse," and in the soliloquy of Beatrice, " O beaux rêves évanouis." The love duet is scarcely on the same level. It begins well, but the climax, sung by the two voices in unison, is rather too conventional in style.

Before taking leave of this opera mention must be made of the impressive march in the first act accompanying the entry of the Bishop, the Chapter of Notre-Dame, the Sherifs, and various Confraternities. This is conceived in the right vein and suggests the presence of high ecclesiastical functionaries. Its effect when heard in its proper place can well be imagined.

In conclusion, it is permissible to express the hope that one day some impressario may think it worth his while to consider the advisability of rescuing this work from an unmerited neglect. In the meanwhile, the score may be recommended to music lovers, who will find much in its pages to interest them.

HENRY VIII

Opera in four Acts. Words by Léonce Détroyat and Armand Sylvestre. Produced at the Académie Nationale de Musique, Paris, March 5, 1883.

It took Saint-Saëns a long time to reach the stronghold of opera in Paris, the gorgeous edifice due to the constructive genius of the architect Garnier, yclept Académie Nationale de Musique and more familiarly known as the Grand Opéra. Hitherto he had been almost a stranger to the operatic public of Paris, although of course well known in the concert-room through his many instrumental works, his two most important operas *Samson and Delilah* and *Étienne Marcel* not having yet reached the capital. The greatest interest had naturally been aroused by the tardy appearance in the great opera house of a work by one who had already acquired so great a European reputation. Neither were the most sanguine expectations destined to be disappointed, for *Henry VIII* obtained a great and deserved success.

In selecting our much-married monarch as the hero of this opera the authors of the book did not evidently trouble much about historical accuracy. The story upon which they concocted their libretto may be summarized in a few words.

Henry has fallen in love with Anne Boleyn, who also has an admirer in the Spanish ambassador Don Gomez, and endeavours to procure his divorce from Katharine of Aragon. The Papal legate refuses to grant the divorce, upon which the King publicly breaks with the Church of Rome. The marriage with Anne Boleyn having taken place, Henry's jealousy is aroused, and he suspects his wife of caring for the Spanish Ambassador. Katharine, weak and ill, is now living in retirement at Kimbolton, and possesses a compromising letter from Anne to Don Gomez, which Henry is anxious to obtain. The King, therefore, visits his first wife accompanied by Don Gomez, while Anne arrives on a similar quest. The situation which follows, as may be imagined, is of a very thrilling character, and furnishes the most harrowing scene in the opera. In order to excite the revengeful feelings of Katharine and force her to give him the letter, Henry displays his love for Anne in the most ardent manner possible. Katharine, however, resists the temptation to harm her rival. She throws the letter into the fire, gradually becomes weaker, and dies without divulging the secret. Henry, who is evidently unconvinced, remarks that if he should ever find out that he has been deceived he will have recourse to the axe, and so ends the opera.

It is scarcely necessary to point out the defects of such a distortion of history, for which librettists have never shown much respect. Sufficient is it to recognize that the plot and its setting offer the composer plenty of scope for varied musical treatment.

The characters are not particularly interesting in themselves. The only one who commands any sympathy is the unhappy Katharine. The cruel sensualism of Henry makes him a particularly repellent personage, Anne appears as an ambitious coquette, and Don Gomez rather a vapid sort of hero. The great scene in which the schism from the Roman Church is pronounced furnishes a situation not unlike that at the end of the first act of *L'Africaine*, so effectively treated by Meyerbeer, and Saint-Saëns has successfully contrived to avoid undue comparison with this.

The opera is preceded by a prelude the theme of which is taken from an old English manuscript, and a characteristic note is struck at the outset. This same theme produces a great effect in the scene of the Synod, when it is sung by the populace after Henry has refused to submit to the Pope's decree. The first act contains an expressive song for the King, " Qui donc commande quand il aime," and a dramatic duet between him and Katharine. A particularly striking episode follows. The King, deaf to the entreaties of his Queen, has sentenced his favourite Buckingham to death. In the distance may be heard a funeral dirge, and the tones of the " De Profundis " strike terror into the hearts of the courtiers who crowd the window to witness the procession to the scaffold. Henry, in the meanwhile, is whispering ardent words of love into the ears of Anne Boleyn. This scene has been admirably realized by the composer, the contrasts between the sentiments of the various characters being most tellingly accentuated.

The second act includes the great love scene between Henry and Anne, which may be placed on a par with the famous seduction scene in *Samson and Delilah*, and in which the King presses his suit by singing a lovely melody, " De ton regard la douceur me pénètre." In the earlier opera it is the woman who is trying to vanquish the resistance of the man by appealing to his senses, whereas here it is the reverse, the man seeking to obtain possession of a woman who does not care for him by promises of power, position, and wealth. Delilah's seductive accents do not represent her true feelings. Here, on the contrary, Henry is so much in earnest that he is ready to sacrifice everything in order to gratify his passion.

Katharine, in a touching scene, endeavours in vain to stop Anne on her downward course. The Papal legate now arrives. According to the traditions of the Paris Opéra the introduction of a ballet is obligatory, so Henry is made to offer this dignitary the pleasure of witnessing a series of Scottish dances at Richmond. When the opera was played at Covent Garden this ballet was omitted, possibly as constituting too great an outrage on historical accuracy. It forms a charming Suite, and in this way has often been heard in concert-rooms.

A pompous and striking march opens the scene of the Synod, in which the choral masses are tellingly employed. The last act is divided into two tableaux, the second of which is constructed in a masterly manner. Katharine sings a sad complaint in which she laments her fate and pines for her native land. Anne Boleyn enters veiled. After a short while the rivals are joined by the King and Don Gomez. The final Quartet, deeply emotional and stirringly dramatic, worthily brings the opera to an end.

It is emphatically to the composer's credit that he should have treated a difficult subject in so admirable a fashion, for the score of *Henry VIII* teems with musical beauties of a very high order, and is interesting from more than one point of view.

At the time of its production it was keenly discussed, and furnished matter for arguments concerning the eternal question revolving around the technique of the modern musical drama as opposed to the older and more conventional opera. The opinions expressed were on the whole favourable to the composer, whose skill was universally praised, although he was criticized for attempting to combine two opposite methods of treatment, and while using his orchestra symphonically according to the Wagnerian theory, that is, by employing representative themes, retaining certain operatic formulas of the past.

That a symphonist like Saint-Saëns should be actuated by the desire to make his orchestra take its proper part in suggesting the psychology of the drama is but natural. His treatment of leading themes has little in common with that of Wagner. Always perfectly straightforward and clear in the expression of his thoughts, he has put into practice in all his operatic works the advice he once gave to composers, that they should belong to their country and to their time.

PROSERPINE

Lyrical Drama in four Acts. Words by Louis Gallet (after a play by Auguste Vacquerie). Produced at the Opéra-Comique, Paris, March 15, 1887.

Saint-Saëns' next opera partakes of a melodramatic character and has no connection with mythology, as might be imagined from the title. The story, the action of which is laid in Italy during the sixteenth century, is not a pleasant one. It deals with the love

of Proserpine, a courtesan, for Sabatino, a young noble-
man who is engaged to be married to Angiola, the
sister of his friend Renzo. With the aid of a bandit
named Squarocca, Proserpine tries in vain to harm the
lovers. Finally, after passionately declaring her love
to Sabatino, maddened by jealousy she strikes Angiola
with her stiletto. Sabatino snatches the weapon from
her hand and kills her. This dénouement was not
considered satisfactory. In a later version of the opera
Proserpine is stopped by Sabatino when she is trying
to stab Angiola, upon which she plunges the weapon
into her own breast and dies.

In his setting of this unsavoury story Saint-Saëns
was faithful to the system he had already employed
in *Henry VIII* of making a moderate use of leading
themes. The general texture of the music is remarkable for the same excellence of workmanship shown in
the previous opera, and the dramatic situations are
powerfully treated.

The gem of the work is the finale to the second act,
the scene of which is laid in a convent, where a number
of mendicants have entered to receive alms. The
peaceful atmosphere of the place has been realized to
perfection by the composer. A haunting melodic
figure softly accompanies the voices, and the effect is
quite enchanting. At the first performance this finale
had to be repeated. Unfortunately the two last acts,
in which the language is sometimes too crudely realistic,
did not produce an equally favourable impression.

Whether the opera will be revived and given a chance
of acquiring popularity it is impossible to say. One
critic, Étienne Destranges, considered it the composer's
best work after *Samson and Delilah*, and wrote an interest-

ing pamphlet in which he analysed the score minutely
and labelled the various leading themes employed
therein.

ASCANIO

Opera in five Acts. Words by Louis GALLET (after the
drama *Benvenuto Cellini*, by PAUL MEURICE). Produced at
the Académie Nationale de Musique, Paris, March 5, 1890.

The story which furnished the plot of the composer's
next opera is far more satisfactory, although rather
involved and in parts too melodramatic. The centre
figure is that of Benvenuto Cellini. The reason why
the famous artist's name was not adopted as the title
of the work was out of respect for Berlioz, who had
written an opera so termed many years before.

Benvenuto, who is always striving to reproduce in
marble what he calls *l'éternelle beauté*, thinks that he
has at last discovered his ideal in Colombe, the daughter
of the Provost of Paris. Unfortunately this young
lady is also loved by Ascanio, Benvenuto's favourite
pupil. Further complications arise from the fact that
Benvenuto's admiration for Colombe has stirred the
jealousy of Scozzone, a young Italian girl who is
devoted to him. To make matters worse, a violent
passion for Ascanio has been aroused in the breast of
the Duchesse d'Etampes, a high lady of the Court of
Francis I.

The two discarded ladies determine to revenge
themselves upon the unfortunate Colombe, and adopt
a singular method to rid themselves of their rival.
Benvenuto, who has discovered the love existing between
Ascanio and Colombe, has nobly retired and left the
field to his younger rival. In order to shelter Colombe

from danger he decides to hide her in a reliquary he has constructed for the Ursuline nuns and have her transported therein to the convent. The Duchess, hearing of this, arranges for the reliquary to be taken to her own house and kept there long enough for Colombe to be suffocated. Scozzone, however, repenting of her share in the projected crime, makes up her mind to save Colombe and sacrifices her own life by taking her place in the fatal reliquary. As a reward for his new masterpiece Benvenuto asks the King to consent to the marriage of Colombe and Ascanio. The Duchess then opens the reliquary and, in the place of her rival, finds that she has killed her best friend. Benvenuto, in despair, bids farewell to gaiety, light, and love. So ends this curious story, which undoubtedly possesses a strong human interest, though the plot is rather far-fetched and over-complicated.

In spite of its tragic ending, the general tone of the work is not too strenuous and is indeed rather bright than otherwise. The brilliant period in which it takes place furnishes an opportunity for the most lavish display of the costumier's art. Then, with the exception of the wicked Duchess and her accomplice, one Pagolo, the characters are all more or less sympathetic.

Benvenuto's generous self-abnegation, Scozzone's devotion, Ascanio's chivalrous nature, Colombe's virginal purity, are such as to appeal directly to the feelings. One cannot help regretting that it should have been thought advisable to end the work so tragically. It would surely not have been difficult to allow Scozzone to recover, and all might have terminated with a song of general rejoicing, the Duchess being left gnashing her teeth in impotent fury! Whether

5

this ending would have ensured a more permanent success to the opera it is impossible to say. Certain it is that at the outset it received so flattering a reception that one might have imagined it had come to stay. Yet after the year of its production, when it was played some thirty times, it was given again the following year, since when it has been left severely alone.

Saint-Saëns' score deserved a far better fate, for it is certainly one of the best he has contributed to the operatic stage. Nowhere has he displayed a more intimate sense of the alliance of music and words, and nowhere has he revealed greater sensitiveness in the treatment of tender and emotional situations.

To praise the admirable workmanship that shows itself in every detail of the opera would be superfluous, for it may be taken for granted in the case of one for whom operatic technique has no secrets. But one feels that in *Ascanio* the composer found a subject which appealed to him particularly, and that he threw himself heart and soul into translating the emotions of the various characters into music.

Shortly after the production of this opera there appeared an enthusiastic appreciation of it written by no less a musician than Gounod. In the course of this, the composer of *Faust* cautions one against thinking that it is possible to form a correct idea of the value of the opera by simply reading the piano score, although this has been prepared by the composer himself: " One must hear the work at the theatre, and this for two chief reasons : the first is that a number of musical intentions only find their verification, their sanction, on the stage ; the second, that the richness and the constant interest of the instrumentation cast over the entire work an incomparable prestige and an indispensable complement to the dramatic expression."

These remarks would apply to most modern operas, but as *Ascanio* has been so unaccountably neglected by managers, there is no other possibility for music lovers to become acquainted with its beauties than through the medium of the piano score.

The brighter portions of the opera have been treated with a wonderfully light touch, and the music sparkles ever alert and brilliant with iridescent hues. The composer has also displayed tenderness and emotion in the more serious scenes. If the music does not harrow the feelings too deeply, it is often touching and always well in accord with the situations. There is an occasional suggestion of Hans Sachs in Benvenuto, both characters being imbued with a somewhat similar feeling of self-sacrifice.

It would serve no purpose to single out various portions of this most interesting score, but attention may be drawn to the tender love passages between Ascanio and Colombe, and also to the emotional accents of Benvenuto, particularly in the scene when he realizes that the love he pines for is not his, and he generously retires before his younger and more favoured rival. The words *Enfants je ne vous en veux pas* are expressed in the most simple fashion, yet with real emotional feeling. That fine artist Jean Lassalle, who had previously achieved a great success as Henry VIII, was a superb Benvenuto. Those who witnessed his impersonation of Hans Sachs in the Italian production of *Meistersinger* at Covent Garden many years ago will easily realize how fitted he must have been to interpret such a part.

Before laying aside the score of *Ascanio* mention must

be made of the ballet music, replete with archaic charm, in which Saint-Saëns has reproduced certain characteristics of the music of the period.

PHRYNÉ

Opéra-Comique in two Acts. Words by L. Augé de Lassus.
Produced at the Opéra-Comique, Paris, May 24, 1893.

After dealing with so many tragic events, Saint-Saëns must evidently have felt the desire of displaying the lighter side of his dramatic talent. At a moment when the musical Press was filled with dissertations on the value or non-value of the *leit motiv* and the newer forms of the musical drama, when the works of Wagner were gradually finding their way on to the Paris boards, when Verdi, by producing his *Falstaff*, was ending his glorious stage career with a gigantic burst of laughter, the French master quietly and unobtrusively brought out a short work containing dialogue, and so conforming to the traditions of the Opéra-Comique, simple, refined, and quite individual in style, but making no pretence whatever to novelty of structure. Those who expected him to produce a comedy in music which would have been a French equivalent to the *Meistersinger* or *Falstaff* were disappointed. Certainly Saint-Saëns had shown in *Ascanio* and other operas that he was essentially the composer fitted to attempt such a task. He preferred, however, to confine himself to a work of more modest pretensions, one which he must have written with comparative ease and doubtless with pleasure.

The libretto might have incurred the disapproval of Mrs. Grundy had this good lady seen it, but it is bright and amusing. The beautiful courtesan Phryné has a young lover named Nicias, whose uncle, an old magistrate,

has also fallen a victim to her charms. She makes fun
of her senile admirer and has no difficulty in turning
him into ridicule. There is no necessity to enter into
a description of the laughable situations which naturally
follow. The public of the Opéra-Comique gave a warm
reception to this attractive little work, which obtained
a considerable number of representations at the time.
The title-rôle was enacted by the lovely Miss Sybil
Saunderson, whose statuesque figure rendered her
particularly fitted to impersonate a classical beauty.

FRÉDÉGONDE

Opera in five Acts, left unfinished by ERNEST GUIRAUD
and completed by SAINT-SAËNS. Produced at the Académie
Nationale de Musique, December 18, 1896.

To complete an unfinished opera by another composer
is a most ungrateful task, and it must have been from a
sense of loyalty to the memory of his friend Ernest
Guiraud, who had died in 1892, that Saint-Saëns undertook it. Guiraud, who was an extremely able writer
for the orchestra, had apparently only set three acts of
this opera, and even these had to be scored by his pupil
Paul Dukas, while Saint-Saëns took entire charge of the
last acts. A work constructed in this manner was unlikely
to possess sufficient unity to prove permanently successful.
Although well received, *Frédégonde* disappeared after eight
performances.

LES BARBARES

Lyrical Tragedy in three Acts and a Prologue. Words by
VICTORIEN SARDOU and P. B. GHEUSI. Produced at the
Académie Nationale de Musique, October 23, 1901.

This work had originally been intended for performance
in the open-air theatre of the town of Orange, where the

action of the piece is laid ; this intention, however, had
to be abandoned.   The tragic plot, of which the following
is a summary, is simple, straightforward, and unencum-
bered by too many extraneous details.

The town of Orange has been invaded by Teutonic
hordes and is about to be given over to pillage, when
Marcomir, their chief, is struck by the beauty of Floria,
the priestess of Vesta, and in order to win her love
consents to spare the inhabitants and to withdraw his
soldiers.   Floria, after a short struggle, agrees to belong
to the conqueror.   It appears that the Roman consul
Euryalus has been killed in battle by an unknown man.
Livia, his widow, finds out that the one who has slain him
is no other than Marcomir, whom she stabs with a piece
of the weapon she had extracted from her husband's body.

The score written by Saint-Saëns on this subject is
notable for its unity of style.   Following the method
adopted in his previous operas, he has here applied the
system of representative themes perhaps to an even
greater extent.   The music is imbued with a spirit of
classical simplicity which accords well with the subject
it illustrates, although the composer's inspiration does
not always remain on the same level.   A long and
elaborate overture, which was heard in London at the
Queen's Hall under the composer's direction in 1902,
precedes the opera.   This takes the form of a Symphonic
Prologue during which a narrator explains how " a
century before Christ Rome trembled.   Against her,
300,000 Germans, giants with red hair, descended
suddenly from the misty North, and hurled themselves
against the legions."

Les Barbares did not enjoy a long life on the boards
of the Opéra, and so far has not been revived.

HÉLÈNE

Lyrical Poem in one Act. Words and music by CAMILLE
SAINT-SAËNS. Produced February 18, 1904, at Monte Carlo.

In the present instance the master did not rely on
the assistance of professional librettists, but elected to
write his own poem, choosing as his heroine Helen of
Troy, the story of whose flight with Pâris, the son of
Priam, so fraught with tragic consequences, is presented
in one act divided into seven tableaux.

The first scene is laid outside the palace of Menelaus
at night-time, when voices are heard singing the praises
of the Doric King, his wife Helen, and their guest
Pâris. In the next scene we are at the seaside, where
Helen, who is consumed by an internal fire, arrives
in a weeping condition to ask the gods to help her to
escape from the love of Pâris. Her prayers being
unanswered, she tries to end her existence. As she is
about to throw herself into the sea she is arrested by
the appearance of Aphrodite, surrounded by nymphs,
who gives her very bad advice and bids her to listen
to the voice of Love, predicting for her the glory her
beauty will obtain in future years. At that opportune
moment arrives Pâris, who ardently presses his suit.
Helen, however, still resists and prays to her father
Zeus for help in her trouble. Dark clouds now cover
the horizon, and a clap of thunder heralds the appearance of Pallas, who comes as a messenger from Zeus,
the master of destinies. She warns the lovers of the
terrible consequences that will follow if they give way
to their illicit passion, and shows them a vision of Troy
in flames, with the butchered heroes, Priam and his
sons, including Pâris, all meeting with a violent end.

Undeterred by this terrible spectacle, Pâris declares himself ready to sacrifice his country, his father, and himself, sooner than give up Helen, upon which Pallas solemnly bids him to follow his destiny. Helen defends herself no longer. Carried away by the example of Pâris, she is now equally ready to abandon home, husband, and country for his sake. Darkness has vanished, the sky now is radiantly blue, and the two lovers with their arms entwined, oblivious of the world, depart, and are seen later on in the distance sailing away in a ship towards Troy.

The all-absorbing power of love is therefore the leading idea permeating the work. The music to suggest such a passion would need to be of a richly enveloping type, to flow in torrential waves of lava, all-embracing, burning, consuming, destroying! This is scarcely what the composer has aimed at achieving. His work, which consists of a kaleidoscopic succession of scenes, though it affords great opportunities to the scenic artist, suggests the cantata rather than the opera.

In composing the music, Saint-Saëns has evidently desired to charm rather than to astonish. His score is a model of elegance and grace, and through its exquisite refinement and perfect finish is more calculated to appeal to the few than to the many. By the simplicity and nobility of the declamation it is sometimes suggestive of Gluck. The music allotted to Venus and her nymphs is extremely seductive, while the apparition of Pallas is depicted in appropriately sombre colours. The chief melody of the love scene is not devoid of charm, if perhaps scarcely distinctive enough to be employed in connection with so absorbing a passion.

Altogether, in *Hélène*, one seems to be assisting at an

incident of Homeric times depicted with the pencil of a musical miniaturist. Some might consider that for a subject dealing with gods, goddesses, and heroic characters the music was of too intimate a nature. It pursues its course so calmly, and its emotion is never allowed to become too strenuous. These lovers express themselves in the most polished accents, and the magnitude of their passion has about it a certain classical decorum. In this respect it offers a decided contrast to the vividly emotional operas of recent years. This was very noticeable when the work was performed at Covent Garden in 1904 the same evening as Massenet's *La Navarraise*, no two operas by contemporary composers belonging to the same nation affording a greater contrast one to the other. The title-rôle in *Hélène* was admirably interpreted by Mme Melba, but the work was not given sufficiently often to make a permanent impression.

L'ANCÊTRE

Lyrical Drama in three Acts. Words by Augé de Lassus.
Produced at Monte Carlo, February 24, 1906.

This opera met with success on its original production in the beautiful Principality of Monaco and also at the Paris Opéra-Comique, where it was given some five years later. The action takes place in Corsica at the time of the first Empire, and, as a matter of course, deals with a vendetta.

We have here another version of the story of *Romeo and Juliet*. The Capulets and the Montagues in this instance bear the names of Fabiani and Nera. The feud between the two families has existed for years.

The hermit Raphael, a holy man who lives by the cultivation of bees and flowers, has decided to try and reconcile the two families. In order to do this he summons them to meet, and finds that they are ready to forget their old quarrels. The only one who holds out is Nunciata, the ancestress, who refuses to bury the hatchet. It must be mentioned that Tebaldo Nera is in love with Margarita, the foster-sister of Vanina Fabiani. When the body of Leandri, the brother of Vanina, is brought in and it is found that he has been shot, the ancestress Nunciata insists that an oath of extermination be taken against the hereditary enemies of their family. Vanina, who happens also to be in love with Tebaldo, after some hesitation agrees to take this oath.

On a beautiful sunny day Margarita is plucking roses and thinking of Tebaldo, who has been denounced to Vanina by Bursica, her swineherd, as being the murderer of Leandri. The hermit reproaches Tebaldo for having committed the murder. Tebaldo, however, justifies himself by explaining that he only did it in self-defence. This being so, the hermit blesses the union of Tebaldo and Margarita in the chapel.

The terrible ancestress wants Vanina to avenge the murder of Leandri by killing Tebaldo. Vanina agrees to do so, and takes the gun handed to her by Nunciata, but her love being greater than her jealousy, she lets it fall. The grim old lady, however, does not mean to forego her revenge, so she determines to undertake it herself, and rushes after Tebaldo and Margarita. Two gunshots are heard, but it is Vanina who has been struck and who dies in the arms of Bursica to save the life of the one she loves.

Although there is nothing very new in a plot which owes a good deal to Shakespeare's *Romeo* and to Prosper Mérimée's *Colomba*, yet it forms an excellent subject for operatic treatment. In his setting of the sombre and picturesque story Saint-Saëns has displayed an astonishing amount of vigour and dramatic power, besides a veritably youthful inspiration. His music follows faithfully and illustrates graphically all the varied and contrasting scenes of the drama. In describing the calm existence of the excellent hermit, or in painting the feelings of hatred expressed by the dreaded ancestress, he never fails to realize the desired effect. The love passages between Margarita and Tebaldo are fresh and charming. Throughout the work it may be said that action and music are in perfect accord. It is surprising that so interesting an opera should not have found its way to England. *L'Ancêtre* certainly occupies a special place in the composer's dramatic output.

DÉJANIRE

Lyrical Tragedy in four Acts. Words by LOUIS GALLET and C. SAINT-SAËNS. Produced at Monte Carlo, March 14, 1911.

Saint-Saëns had written an important score for a drama by Louis Gallet bearing the above title and destined to be performed in the open air in the arenas of Béziers, where it was played with great success in 1898. Having been asked to write another opera for Monte Carlo, the master conceived the idea of adapting this work for the operatic stage. His friend and collaborator, Louis Gallet, having died, he took the matter in hand himself, made certain alterations in the text, and set the whole to music. In its new form the work was first heard on the sunny shores of the Mediterranean, and in the month of November the same year was played at the Paris Opéra.

The composer has related himself how the first version of the piece came to be written. In 1897 he was visiting the arenas of Béziers, where Louis Gallet wanted to have a work performed, but was doubting whether this should take the form of a tragedy or an opera. Saint-Saëns decided in favour of a tragedy, with choruses intervening after the manner of the old Greek drama.

Mythology has proved a happy hunting-ground for composers, and Saint-Saëns seems to have been particularly attracted by Hercules, whose personality is already suggested in two of his Symphonic Poems (*Le Rouet d'Omphale* and *La Jeunesse d'Hercule*), while in the present instance he figures as the chief male character.

The opera deals with the culminating event in the legendary hero's career. The author of the words had evidently studied Sophocles with profit. The heroine is the wife of Hercules, and, being of a jealous disposition, takes effectual means to calm her husband's amorous instincts.

The legend has it that a tunic steeped in the blood of the centaur Nessus, which she sent to her spouse and which he unwisely wore, caused him the greatest agony and finally killed him. Hercules was placed on a superb funeral pyre and, whilst this was burning, was carried away to Olympus and became a god.

To typify Hercules, Saint-Saëns has employed the fine theme which figures prominently in his Symphonic Poem, *La Jeunesse d'Hercule*. The score of *Déjanire* is nobly conceived and is notable for strength and

expressiveness. That clarity of writing associated with
the composer is very uncommon at a time when musicians
are going to the backs of their heads in their search for
excruciating chords and startling effects !

Although well received at the Paris Opéra, the work
does not appear to have proved sufficiently attractive
to remain in the répertoire.

The different examples of ballet music included in the
operas of Saint-Saëns prove the master's aptitude in
dealing with the various forms of dance music. A
charming one-act ballet from his pen entitled *Javotte*
was produced with success at Lyons in 1896, and at the
Paris Opéra-Comique on October 23, 1899. It was
transferred to the boards of the Grand Opéra on
February 5, 1909.

The composer's connection with the stage does not,
however, end here, for he has also contributed incidental
music to *Antigone*, a tragedy by Paul Meurice and Auguste
Vacquerie, after Sophocles.

Two important scores have also been furnished by
him for Louis Gallet's *Déjanire* and Mme Jane Dieulafoy's *Parysatis*, both produced in the arenas of Béziers.
The first of these works, as mentioned previously, was
later on elaborated by the composer and turned to
operatic account. If space were not limited, it would
be pleasant to allude at greater length to these works.
By reason of the peculiar circumstances which called
them into existence they demand a locale for their
performance not easily to be found.

The foregoing remarks on the operas of Saint-Saëns
should suffice to give an idea of the enormous pro-

ductivity of the composer when it is remembered that, in England at all events, his reputation rests mainly upon other works. There is not one among the operas I have mentioned which is devoid of interest. They all reveal the hand of a master craftsman, and if they are not all equally interesting this is not surprising, and may in some instances be attributed to the librettists and also to the fact that inspiration is not always at a composer's beck and call, be he ever so great.

To have written an opera like *Samson and Delilah*, which has obtained a world success, is a sufficient achievement in itself. Yet it seems a great pity that the other operas of Saint-Saëns should be so neglected. *Henry VIII*, for instance, was performed here at Covent Garden two or three times in 1898, but has not been revived, so that the public has never had a chance of appreciating its great merits. Then *Étienne Marcel*, *Proserpine*, *Ascanio*, *L'Ancêtre*, have not been heard here at all, which is extremely regrettable.

It is difficult to understand why certain operas should attract whilst others, equally good in their way, should not. In some cases it is the fault of the musician, and in others of the librettist. Given an interesting subject allied to good music, and success would seem assured. This, however, is by no means invariably the case. The operas that have acquired a really world-wide fame during the last fifty or sixty years are comparatively few in numbers. On the other hand, many have started well, but have gradually dropped out of favour, while others have only maintained their position in the country of their birth.

For instance, Gounod's *Mireille* has remained a favourite in France, but is never heard now in England.

Again, Massenet's *Werther* is decidedly popular in Paris, but never had any success over here, even when the name part was taken by Jean de Reszke! The same may be said of Lalo's *Le Roi d'Ys* and of other operas.

If we go back to the past we are confronted by many curious instances illustrating the impossibility of assigning any good reason for the survival of certain works and the disappearance of others. Certain operas survive mainly through the grace of the almighty prima donna. Otherwise why should Donizetti's *Lucia di Lammermoor* remain while his *Lucrezia Borgia* is forgotten? Yet the latter is quite as melodious as the former, and has a capital plot.

Some operas suffer a temporary eclipse and, when rediscovered, shine with a renewed splendour. The operas of Meyerbeer are still played on the Continent, and will probably be heard again here when a manager is intelligent enough to realize the effect they produce when properly sung.

In France it constantly happens that an opera which has been given a long period of rest is revived with success. With us the case is different as, up to the present, we depend upon private enterprise for our operatic fare and have no government subventioned opera house. This being so, we look to the concert-room for opportunities of becoming acquainted with works destined for the stage, a very excellent way, be it said, of appreciating the music *per se*.

No better instance of the value of concert performances of operatic music can be given than that relating to Wagner, whose masterpieces have gradually become known mainly through fragmentary performances in concert-rooms. This is all the more remarkable in his case, as it is well known that he was of opinion that to appreciate his music properly it should be heard with all the adjuncts of the stage, etc. Yet who would be prepared to say that the funeral music in *Götterdämmerung* is heard to the same advantage at Covent Garden, half drowned by the sound of the scene-shifters' voices and other disconcerting noises, as it is when played at the Queen's Hall ?

Long before the strange edict against the stage performance of works founded on stories taken from the Bible had been repealed, *Samson and Delilah* had become familiar to our musical public through repeated concert performances. Why then should not the many musical treasures that are buried in the scores of unperformed operas be revealed to the public in a similar manner ? Certainly it may be said that in the case of *Samson and Delilah* the character of the work renders it particularly suitable for performance in the concert-room. On the other hand, other operas—*Faust* and *Cavalleria Rusticana*, for instance—have often been given successfully in this way. Mancinelli's *Hero and Leander* was introduced at a Norwich festival in concert form before being played on the stage at Covent Garden.

It need not always be necessary to perform entire operas, but there is no reason why whole scenes or even acts should not be produced in this manner, as in the case of Wagner's music dramas. There is no doubt that great deal might thus be done to bring before the notice of the public works the very existence of which they ignore. Songs, overtures, or detached pieces constantly figure on programmes, then why not more extended selections ?

In connection with the operas of Saint-Saëns, the

fourth act of *Henry VIII*, the second act of *Proserpine*, an act of *Ascanio*—these and other extracts from his operas would show the British public another side of this composer's talent, one with which they are at present insufficiently familiar, and possibly this might eventually lead to a stage performance of one of these neglected operas.

CHAPTER IV

WORKS FOR ORCHESTRA

(SYMPHONIES, SYMPHONIC POEMS, CONCERTOS, ETC.)

IN the preceding chapter an effort has been made to give an idea of Saint-Saëns as a composer of operas. In the present one he will be considered in connection with concert works written for the orchestra, by which he is better known in England, and which exhibit his genius in several different aspects.

The dual nature of his musical personality, to which allusion has already been made, constantly reveals itself here. He shows himself in turns a respecter of consecrated forms, thus keeping in touch with the famous symphonists of the past, although expressing his thoughts in a more modern language, and an enthusiastic believer in progress.

A thorough adept in the art of musical construction, he has been able to succeed in what is termed " absolute " music as well as in " programme " music. Built on solid classical ground, his symphonic works denote a complete mastery of form, and wherever his fancy takes him he is able to guide it with a sure hand. Thus is it that he has always succeeded in keeping clear of exaggeration and in avoiding, on the one hand, the dull academicism of the pedant and, on the other, the incoherence of the musical mountebank.

We have seen that Saint-Saëns first attracted attention to his name as a composer by the production of a symphony when he was still in his teens. This fact is particularly noteworthy inasmuch as at that time instrumental music based on classical symphonic forms was little cultivated in France. Therefore, it showed both courage and independence on the part of the young musician that he should at the outset of his career have set himself to work on what is perhaps the most difficult and certainly the least encouraged branch of musical composition. It also denoted the serious bent of his mind and demonstrated the influence of the classical masters with whose music he had lived on familiar terms ever since his earliest childhood.

In another chapter it has been related how this Symphony won the approbation of musicians such as Berlioz and Gounod and stamped its author as a composer with a future.

This first Symphony, in E flat, which was produced in 1853 and published two years later, is dedicated to M. Seghers, under whose direction it was first played. It was succeeded by two more symphonies, in 1856 and 1859, neither of which has been published. By composing these works Saint-Saëns was gradually acquiring that sureness of hand and familiarity with the orchestra so notable in all his instrumental compositions.

The Symphony in A minor, which is known as the second, but is really the fourth, dates from 1859, but was not published until 1878, and bears the *opus* number 55. It was given in London at a concert of the Royal Philharmonic Society on June 23, 1898, under the conductorship of the composer.

Essentially classical in its form, the Symphony is divided into the usual four movements and written for a small orchestra without trombones and with only two horns. Perfect limpidity of treatment, soberness of the means employed, and command over contrapuntal devices are points that may be noted. On the other hand, it cannot be pronounced a particularly individual work, and strikes one as being more remarkable for ingenuity than for any real originality of thought. Suggestions of Mozart, Beethoven, and Mendelssohn are frequent. The Scherzo, a bright and attractive movement, pleased the Philharmonic audience so much that it had to be repeated. Still, the Symphony as a whole gives one the impression of a work written as an exercise in a form and style consecrated by time rather than as the expression of deep personal feeling. At the period when it was composed, Saint-Saëns was still quite a young man, and in writing it he was paying a doubtless unconscious homage to the famous masters he admired so much, besides proving once again his ability to model his style more or less upon theirs.

A long time was to elapse between the composition of this Symphony and the next, the now famous Symphony in C minor, with organ. Before enlarging upon the merits of this remarkable work it will be advisable to consider those contributions to the literature of the orchestra which have been the means of popularizing the name of Saint-Saëns at least as much as any of his compositions,

THE SYMPHONIC POEMS

The master has related himself how the Symphonic Poems of Liszt pointed out to him the road he was destined to follow, and which led him to compose works such as the *Danse Macabre* and the *Rouet d'Omphale.* " Not so very long ago," he wrote, " instrumental music had only two forms at its disposal : the Symphony and the Overture. Haydn, Mozart, and Beethoven had not written anything else ; who would have dared to do otherwise ? Neither Weber, nor Mendelssohn, nor Schubert, nor Schumann had ventured to do so. Liszt had the courage to do it." Understanding that in order to impose new forms it was necessary to justify them by making their necessity felt, Liszt had entered resolutely into the road that Beethoven, in the *Pastoral Symphony*, the *Choral Symphony*, Berlioz in the *Fantastic Symphony* and *Harold in Italy*, had indicated rather than opened, for if they had enlarged the framework of the Symphony, they had not broken it, and he created the *Symphonic Poem.*

The enthusiasm of Saint-Saëns for Liszt and his genial creation can now be readily understood, but it must be remembered that forty or fifty years ago the musical world was very divided on the relative merits of " programme " music and " absolute " music, and rooted habits of thought are hard to dislodge. Even at the present time, though most composers have followed the luminous road opened by Liszt, there are probably many people who do not realize the enormous importance of the new departure. Saint-Saëns put the matter into a nutshell when he wrote the following words : " For many people, programme music is a necessarily inferior *genre*. Many things have been written on this subject which I find it impossible to understand. Is the music in itself good or bad ? Everything lies there. Whether it has a programme or not, it will neither be better nor worse."

In the same article Saint-Saëns points out that programme music furnishes the artist with a pretext to explore new paths. Here, indeed, speaks one who is not indissolubly wedded to the past, but who, while retaining his respect for forms that have been consecrated by long usage, is ready and eager to extend the domain of musical art. He succinctly describes the Symphonic Poem in the form given to it by Liszt as generally consisting in " an ensemble of different movements depending on each other, and proceeding from a fundamental idea, these being connected together in the form of one piece. The plan of a musical Poem thus understood can be varied indefinitely."

It is quite natural that a musician like Saint-Saëns should have felt attracted by a form of art offering so many opportunities of displaying not only technical knowledge but also calling into play the imaginative faculties. It may be added that his own contributions to this form of art are essentially individual and have little in common with any of the twelve magnificent Symphonic Poems of Liszt. They are less abstract and more compact in form.

Le Rouet d'Omphale (1871), the first, is one of the most popular works in the concert répertoire and is a musical gem of the first water. The subject it is intended to illustrate has been described by the composer, in a note prefixed to the orchestral score, as being " feminine seduction, the triumphant struggle of weakness over strength," the spinning-wheel serving as a pretext, " chosen only for the sake of rhythm, and to give a special character to the piece."

The old legend of Hercules at the feet of Omphale, alluded to by Victor Hugo in his *Contemplations*, is well known. It is the eternal tale of the strong man succumbing to the coquettish charm of a lovely woman. Hercules has to confess himself beaten, and we are led to suppose that Omphale, conscious of her triumph, after laughing at him relents and finishes by not proving too obdurate.

Music seemingly spun with silken threads and embroidered into a texture of iridescent hues envelops this fascinating old fable in a bright and variegated tone garment. Exquisite taste and refinement, finesse and delicacy, render this piece a veritably unique work of [its kind. There is no straining after effect, no exaggeration; all is perfectly limpid and crystal clear. The instruments are treated with love, and every note tells.

The delightful, and slightly impertinent, theme which characterizes the heroine pursues its course fluently with ever-varying charm. There is no mis- taking the theme intended to depict the anguish of Hercules grovelling at the feet of the enchantress. Arising from the depths of the orchestra, it pants and struggles onwards, the expression of unsatisfied longing, until the poor hero owns himself beaten. Then comes a most telling episode, a mocking version of the same theme played by the oboe depicting Omphale laughing at the vain efforts of the strong man. Perhaps the most beautiful effect of a gradual *diminuendo* occurs at the end of the work. The movement of the spinning-wheel is suggested by the violins, punctuated by short chords allotted to the wood wind and horns and finally to the harp and wood wind (flutes and oboes). As the end approaches, the violins are left playing alone, the movement slackens, and the music gradually evaporates on a high harmonic A played by the first violins.

Phaeton (1873), the second of the master's Symphonic Poems, is also inspired by a mythological tale. As in the case of the *Rouet d'Omphale*, the gist of this is given in a prefatory note in the orchestral score.

Phaeton, having obtained permission to drive the chariot of his father, the Sun, in the sky, finds himself unable to control the steeds. The flaming chariot, thrown out of its course, is approaching the terrestrial regions. The entire universe is threatened with destruction, when Jupiter hurls a thunderbolt at the imprudent Phaeton.

A wonderful example of tone-painting, the music may be said to tell its own tale. Even to anyone unacquainted with the story it is intended to illustrate, it would suggest a breathless ride through space, resulting in a catastrophe.

Attention is arrested by four striking introductory bars in which trumpets and trombones conjure up a vision of the glowing Orb, while upward scale passages first for the strings and then the wood wind depict the restlessness of the steeds. A short chord played by the entire orchestra and the start is made. The first theme of the Allegro, agitated and strongly rhythmical, is thoroughly appropriate to describe a wild ride, while the second, sharp and incisive, doubtless stands for the venturesome youth.

Phaeton, after his rapid start, appears now to be

handling the reins with greater ease. The music becomes quieter, and a noble theme of majestic character, allotted to the four horns and evidently emblematical of the Sun, conveys a feeling of calm, reposeful grandeur, the movement of the chariot being suggested by the same rhythmical figure heard previously and now softly accentuated by the violins. Phaeton evidently feels very pleased, for his erstwhile fiery theme assumes a dreamy character. While he is apparently indulging in a rêverie, his steeds suddenly become restive, and he vainly endeavours to regain control over them. The music throbs with agitation and Phaeton's theme assumes despairing accents. The climax is now at hand, and soon Jove's thunderbolt, depicted by the united voices of the orchestra strengthened by the gong and other instruments of percussion, settles the doom of the imprudent youth. The strains die off little by little, and the fine theme representing the Sun is heard once more, lamenting the fate of poor Phaeton.

This brilliant and imaginative work is scored for the usual full orchestra, including two pairs of kettledrums, with a double bassoon *ad lib.*

In his next Symphonic Poem, Saint-Saëns abandoned classical and mythological lore and sought his subject in the grim environments of the churchyard. The *Danse Macabre* was suggested by some verses by Henri Cazalis [1] which the composer had set to music:

> " Zig et Zig et Zig, la Mort en cadence
> Frappant une tombe avec son talon,
> La Mort à minuit joue un air de danse
> Zig et Zig et Zag, sur son violon.

---

[1] Poems published under the pseudonym of Jean Lahor.

> Le vent d'hiver souffle, et la nuit est sombre;
> Des gémissements sortent des tilleuls;
> Les squelettes blancs vont à travers l'ombre,
> Courant et sautant sous leurs grands linceuls.
>
> Zig et Zig et Zig, chacun se trémousse,
> On entend claquer les os des danseurs.
> .   .   .   .   .   .
>
> Mais psit! tout à coup on quitte la ronde,
> On se pousse, on fuit, le coq a chanté."
> .   .   .   .   .   .

This weird theme has inspired the composer to write a work of striking originality, and one which has contributed in no small degree to popularize his name. The grim notion of associating with dancing so sad and solemn a subject as the tomb had already been exploited by Meyerbeer in the famous scene of the resurrection of the nuns in *Robert le Diable*. The term *Danse Macabre* had also been employed by Liszt to describe his fantastic Variations on the *Dies Iræ* for piano and orchestra. In the present work, however, Saint-Saëns has struck out a path for himself.

Midnight sounds, the twelve strokes being played by the harp supported by a horn on the same note, while soft chords for the violins enter on the fourth bar, conveying a glamour of mystery. The witching hour having sounded, the call to the dance is given by the shrill tones of a solo violin, the E string of which has been tuned a half a tone lower. The diminished fifth sounded on the open strings produces a novel and decidedly weird effect. The spectral waltz now begins, at first quietly, then gradually increasing in vivacity, the clattering of bones being realistically suggested by the employment of a xylophone. Unhealthy night breezes sweep around the dancers, a species of parodied version of the *Dies Iræ* is played by the wood wind and harp, then a plaintive wail from the solo violin seems to express the hopelessness of the phantom crew. The frenzied dancing is at its height when suddenly is heard the crowing of a cock, personified by the oboe, heralding the arrival of dawn. This signal breaks the spell, and the dancers scatter hurriedly to their abodes under the ground. A sigh of regret from the solo violin, and all is over.

In his fourth and last Symphonic Poem, *La Jeunesse d'Hercule* (1877), the composer once again turned to mythology. The following description of the subject of the work is prefixed to the full score.

" The fable relates that at the beginning of his life, Hercules saw two roads opening before him : that of pleasure and that of virtue. Insensible to the seductions of nymphs and bacchantes, the hero enters the path of strife and combat, at the end of which he foresees, through the flames of the stake, the reward of immortality."

La Jeunesse d'Hercule is the most ambitious of the four Symphonic Poems, the theme being one which demands a more elaborate treatment, but it is perfectly clear in design and logically constructed, while its significance as a musical interpretation of the subject is never veiled.

The soft flowing passage for the violins with which the work commences heralds appropriately the dawn of the hero's life. It is soon succeeded by the principal theme of the work, which is doubtless intended to typify his moral strength and power of resistance. Saint-Saëns was evidently very fond of this theme, for he employed it many years later in his opera *Déjanire*, also in connection with Hercules. Simple and impressive in its square-cut form, it suitably expresses his intention. Presently voluptuous strains indicate the arrival of nymphs and bacchantes, who endeavour to induce the hero to join them in their pleasures. A veritable bacchanalian orgy now follows, and the music suggests the wildest antics. Hercules, who has apparently yielded to the fascinations of the nymphs and joined in the frenzied revelry, suddenly pulls himself together. His theme acquires fresh power, asserting his conquest over the debilitating influences of unrestricted licence, and the work concludes with the vision of the funeral pyre which is to serve as a prelude to his final apotheosis.

Thus ends one of the most individual compositions of Saint-Saëns. Scored in a masterly manner, it affords a splendid example of his qualities at their best.

Notwithstanding the great success of his four Symphonic Poems, Saint-Saëns does not seem to have been tempted to add to their number, preferring to devote his attention to other forms of music.

An anterior work, which might in a sense be termed a Tone Poem, is the "Marche Héroïque," Op. 34, dedicated to the memory of his friend, the painter, Henri Regnault (1843–71), killed during the Siege of Paris in the dark days of 1871. There is nothing in this work which resembles a Funeral March of the conventional sort. Simply constructed in march form, with an episode in three-four time, and working up to a spirited climax, it is less elegiac in style than expressive of ardour and nervous energy. One can imagine the tramping of a battalion of soldiers eager to repair past defeats and march

to victory. The middle section consists of an impressive
theme first played by a solo trombone, with a delicate
counter-subject for the violins and wood wind, in the
course of which occurs a modulation slightly reminiscent
of a passage in the prison scene of Gounod's *Faust*.
The March is strikingly effective and has long since
become popular.

Saint-Saëns has written two Suites for orchestra.
The first of these is an early work. It was composed
in 1863, though not published until several years later,
is classical in style, has nothing in common with " programme music," and consists of five numbers respectively entitled Prélude, Sarabande, Gavotte, Romance,
and Finale.

The second Suite, on the other hand, belongs to the
picturesque in music, and may be regarded as a tonal
record of the composer's impressions during a sojourn
in sunny Southern climes. It is entitled *Suite Algérienne*
and is also divided into five parts respectively named
Prelude, Rapsodie, Mauresque, Rêverie du Soir, and
Marche Militaire Française.

The Prélude is intended to describe the varied feelings
of the composer on approaching Algiers, and is a vivid
descriptive Tone Picture, effectively blending African
and European musical elements. The Moorish
Rhapsody, as befits its title, is a clever paraphrase of
native tunes. On the other hand, in the languorous
and fascinating Rêverie, the composer transcribes his
own impressions of a lovely moonlight night at Blidah.
The bright and spirited French military March, in the
course of which the composer pays a possibly unconscious
homage to Rossini, brings this attractive Suite to a
conclusion.

Among other contributions by Saint-Saëns to the orchestral concert répertoire may be mentioned a *Rapsodie Bretonne*, founded on an early work for organ on Breton hymns ; a dreamy Barcarolle entitled *Une Nuit à Lisbonne* ; a Sarabande and Rigaudon ; the brilliant March composed for the Coronation of King Edward VII ; and an *Ouverture de Fête*, Op. 133, written in 1909.

SYMPHONY IN C MINOR

There remains to be considered the composer's most important symphonic work, the one which may be said to crown his achievements in instrumental music, the Symphony in C minor, with organ, Op. 78, dedicated to the memory of Franz Liszt and produced for the first time at a concert of the London Philharmonic Society in 1886. Before doing so, a few words concerning the symphonic form and its cultivation in France may not be out of place.

Although the title of " father of the Symphony " is universally attributed to Haydn, yet it is a singular fact that about the same period, 1754, when the genial old master was producing his first Symphony, a work of the same kind was being written in Paris by Gossec (1734–1829), who, though a Belgian by birth, is classed with the composers of France owing to his long residence in Paris. The seed sown by Gossec did not, however, germinate to any great extent in the country of his adoption, the few attempts made by French composers in the succeeding years not amounting to much.

Early in the nineteenth century fresh currents of musical thought were generated on the other side of

the Rhine, and the symphonies of Beethoven gradually
asserted their sway and became known in France.   Then
there appeared a French composer of genius, who was
destined to be one of the chief engineers of musical
progress, Hector Berlioz. This great man, who may
be called the father of modern instrumentation, revolu-
tionized the treatment of the orchestra and expressed
himself in various instrumental works such as the
Fantastic Symphony, *Harold in Italy*, *Romeo and Juliet*,
vast symphonic structures which puzzled the public
of the day, and who wrote the famous treatise on instrumentation which was to prove such a fruitful source
of study to all succeeding composers, and on which he
expended all the exuberance of his poetical imagination.
In later years Berlioz strove vainly to attain the recognition he deserved, but his works were only destined to
meet with success after he had passed away.   In truth
a great artist, soured by ill-success ; a solitary figure
moving in a busy unappreciative commercial age, one
who was ever fighting what appeared to be a losing
battle and who had not the philosophy to bear defeat
with resignation.

Apart from Berlioz, whose symphonies were deeply
impregnated with the romanticism of the epoch, French
composers for a long time seem to have made but fitful
attempts to cultivate this form of music.   Henri Reber's
four Symphonies, symmetrical in structure and imbued
with the spirit of classicism, did not make much headway,
neither did the two written by Gounod add greatly
to the fame of the composer of *Faust*.   The establish-
ment of Pasdeloup's popular concerts of classical music
at the Cirque d'Hiver in 1861 did a great deal to foster
the taste for instrumental music in Paris.   At first

dedicated mainly to classical masterpieces, the scope of
these concerts gradually developed and embraced works
by Wagner and by young and hitherto little-known
French composers. The excellent pioneer work of
Pasdeloup was continued in the seventies by Lamoureux
and Colonne.

During the twenty years that succeeded the Franco-
German War of 1870 several French composers turned
their attention to the Symphony. In 1877 Messager
won the gold medal of the Société des Compositeurs
for a Symphony in four movements, and Fauré wrote
one in 1884 which has never been published. Then
came in quick succession the third Symphony of Saint-
Saëns, one by Lalo, and the famous one by César Franck.
Since that time many French composers have written
symphonies, among them being Chausson and Boëllman,
whose careers were prematurely cut short, Albéric
Magnard, who was killed during the Great War, Paul
Dukas, Vincent d'Indy, Guy Ropartz, etc.

The Symphony, which is the noblest form of instrumental music, is also the most plastic, inasmuch as
the term may be employed in connection with works
differing totally one from the other. The older
symphonies of Haydn and Mozart usually consisted of
four movements, an Allegro sometimes preceded by a
slow introduction, an Adagio, a Minuet, and a Finale.
Beethoven substituted a Scherzo for the Minuet and
otherwise widened the scope of the Symphony, render-
ing it more expressive of human feeling and opening
fresh paths for succeeding composers, who did not fail
to explore them with profit. He also introduced
suggestive elements which previously had not figured
in compositions of this kind, and finally closed his

glorious career by celebrating liberty and adding the
human voice to the orchestra. From that time onwards
the Symphony became more intimately associated with
the expression of feeling. Composers sought through
its medium to do more than merely cut their music
into sections to fit certain ready-made patterns. The
Romantic movement had been started, and has flourished
ever since, despite the curious attitude adopted towards
it of late by certain musicians of futuristic tendencies.
The picturesque, the descriptive, the exotic, and other
elements have been turned to account by some of the
greatest masters of the nineteenth century, while others
have contented themselves with employing the orchestra
as the symphonic interpreter of their own feelings of
happiness or woe.

Thus, if on the one hand we have the pleasant
musical landscapes painted by Mendelssohn and known
as the Italian and Scottish symphonies, the passionate
exuberance of Berlioz expresses itself through the
medium of his Fantastic Symphony, his *Harold in Italy*,
and *Romeo and Juliet*. If Schumann, disdaining any
programme, strives to express his feelings symphonically
and not always so successfully as through the medium
of the piano, Liszt succeeds in commenting the *Faust*
of Goethe and the *Divine Comedy* of Dante in two
so-called symphonies of surprising originality and beauty.
If Raff evokes the charm and mystery of the forest in
one of his symphonies and in another seeks to illustrate
Bürger's famous Ballade and graphically describes the
weird spectral ride of the unhappy Lenore, Brahms
prefers to continue the classical symphonic tradition
in a studiously severe manner. If Rubinstein endeavours
to bring to the mind the mighty ocean in its varied

7

aspects, Tchaikovsky probes the innermost depths of his own heart in his, alas, too prophetic *Pathetic Symphony*. If Brückner, whose works are insufficiently known here, writes a series of remarkable symphonies, in which may be detected the influence both of Beethoven and of Wagner, and if Mahler further experimentalizes in this form, Dvorák employs the characteristic idioms of his own country, and in one famous symphony idealizes the tuneful simplicity of the negro.[1]

That Saint-Saëns, who had shown himself so great a master of the orchestra, should in his full maturity have endeavoured to expand his previous symphonic efforts was inevitable, and the result proved that in so doing he had not overestimated his powers, for the work now under consideration undoubtedly counts among the most remarkable symphonies of modern times.

The third Symphony of Saint-Saëns has no programme. It is dedicated to the memory of Franz Liszt, but it was produced on May 19, 1886, before the great master's death, which occurred the same year on July 31. It has been suggested that the music was intended to describe the romantic career of one who was not only a great composer, but also the most famous of pianists and altogether an exceptionally fascinating personality,

---

[1] This form of music has not been neglected in England during recent years. Sullivan wrote only one Symphony, but Parry left five. Stanford has composed as many as seven, while Cowen and Algernon Ashton have written five each; Elgar, Cliffe, and Edward German two each. Arthur Somervell, Josef Holbrooke, Carse, York Bowen, Farjeon, W. H. Speer, Dunhill, Percy Pitt, Bell, Vaughan Williams, Balfour Gardiner, have also contributed works of this kind to the musical répertoire. This is a pretty good record, but, alas, how many of these works have ever been afforded the opportunity of becoming widely known !

just as Liszt's own splendid Sonata dedicated to
Schumann was supposed to reflect the struggles of the
master of Zwickau. This, however, is immaterial.
That the Symphony possesses a psychological significance
and is not merely to be considered in the light of a
cleverly devised piece of tonal architecture is certain.
Various are the emotions it portrays, from the restlessness and anxiety expressed in the first movement to
the triumphant character of the finale.

The form of the work is unusual. It is divided into
two sections, a proceeding already adopted by the
composer in his fourth pianoforte Concerto and first
violin Sonata. In reality, however, it contains the four
traditional movements, the first leading without break
into the Andante, while the Scherzo likewise is linked
to the Finale. In so constructing his work the composer
has stated that his object was " to avoid the endless
resumptions and repetitions which more and more
tend to disappear from instrumental music under the
influence of increasingly developed musical culture."

The work is built around a leading theme which
appears in a variety of transformations and contains an
evidently intentional suggestion of the *Dies Iræ*.
After a few introductory bars, indicating sadness and
resignation, the Allegro in six-eight time commences
in the minor key, the principal theme being played by
the violins in short staccato notes, somewhat after the
manner of the beginning of Schubert's *Unfinished
Symphony*. The music denotes an agitated and pessi-
mistic frame of mind. The variety of resource exhibited
in the development of the leading theme is admirable.
A second theme of real melodic charm brings with it
a feeling of consolation and hope. After a while the

agitation gradually subsides, and a surprisingly original and striking effect is realized by the manner in which the Allegro merges into the Andante, really the second movement of the Symphony, when the rich tones of the organ support a really beautiful and touching melody played by the strings, expressing a peaceful sense of calm. The first section thus closes in an atmosphere of undisturbed rest.

The dreamy conditions engendered by this lovely Andante are now to be dispelled. A spirit of energy unmistakably asserts itself at the beginning of the second section, and the music becomes fantastic, somewhat after the style of the composer's own *Danse Macabre*, the leading theme undergoing various quaint transformations, while the piano, employed for the sake of certain arpeggio passages, makes an unusual appearance.

The last portion of this monumental work suggests a triumphant optimism and difficulties vanquished. The leading theme at one moment assumes a markedly religious character, while later on it is used as the subject of a fugue. An alluring theme expressive of calm, reposeful joys is also heard, and the Symphony finally ends in the most brilliant and joyful fashion.

In this work the composer has employed a very full orchestra, which includes a cor anglais, bass clarinet, double bassoon, organ, and piano (played sometimes by two, sometimes by four, hands). The introduction of the last two instruments has been criticized as superfluous. As regards the piano, the objection is not illfounded, for the favoured instrument of the household seems rather out of place here, unless its presence be accepted as a reminder that the work is dedicated to the memory of the greatest pianist of all times. On the other hand, the organ evidently has a distinct mission to fulfil in the scheme of the work, and its presence must not be attributed to mere caprice.

Considering that this admirable Symphony, which is considered in France to be the composer's finest instrumental work, was produced for the first time in England, it is more than strange that its performances here should not have been more frequent. It was the principal item on the programme of the Jubilee Festival Concert given at the Queen's Hall on June 2, 1913, in the composer's honour.

CONCERTOS

The Concerto is another form of music in which Saint-Saëns has achieved supreme distinction. He has written five works of this kind with the piano as solo instrument, besides a Fantasia entitled *Africa*, three violin and two violoncello Concertos.

If a pianist were asked to name the most popular Concertos, written since Beethoven, he would doubtless mention Schumann's in A minor, Liszt's in E flat and in A, Tchaikovsky's in B flat minor, Grieg's in A minor, and Saint-Saëns' in G minor and in C minor. He might possibly add Rubinstein's in D minor and Brahms' in the same key, though the latter is rather too recondite in style for universal appreciation.

On June 18, 1887, Saint-Saëns gave an orchestral concert in London at the old St. James's Hall, the disappearance of which is so much to be deplored. This concert, which was conducted by the late Mr. Wilhelm Ganz, commenced with the overture to Weber's *Der Freischütz*, while the remainder of the programme was devoted to the four first Concertos of Saint-Saëns, with the composer as soloist. The occasion will not have been forgotten by those who were present.

The first of the Concertos is an early work and was written in 1859. Classically constructed, it is interesting as the promising effort of a young musician who has not yet developed a style of his own. Very different is the second Concerto, in G minor, Op. 22, which dates from the year 1868, and is one of the most deservedly popular works of its kind. It would be difficult to discover a professional pianist who has not played it, or a regular concert-goer who has not enjoyed hearing it over and over again. Yet it is emphatically one of those works concerning which it may be said that familiarity does *not* breed contempt.

Here we have Saint-Saëns in the plenitude of youth, with a wealth of musical ideas, perfect command over his material, teeming with spirits and unmistakably impressing his own striking personality on his work. At the outset he is grave and solemn, possibly thinking of the organ-loft he has lately occupied ; then he becomes romantic, tender, plaintive, and even passionate. The music of the first movement reveals all these phases of sentiment to me, and is always an unalloyed delight. Then follows the Allegro Scherzando, which has contributed so much to the success of the Concerto. Light, dainty, and frolicsome, it trips merrily along, the absolute musical realization of the joy of living. He would be a very poor creature who could resist the fascination of this enchanting piece, which ripples along so captivatingly, or who would not be impressed by the melodious charm of the second subject. The composer's exuberance of spirits does not flag in the third and last movement, a Presto, which takes the form of a brisk Tarantella and worthily concludes this very delightful work in which inspiration and technical skill are admirably combined.

If the second Concerto has long since acquired a world-wide renown, the same cannot be said of the third, in E flat, Op. 29, and this is very strange considering its great merits. It was written a year later than the previous one, and also consists of three movements. In the place of a Scherzo the composer has included an Andante. The first movement, which begins with a theme reminiscent of Schubert's Symphony in C, is interesting throughout. The Andante, with its lovely melody played by the muted strings, is charming, while the Finale is one of the most exhilarating pieces imaginable, and suggests a frenzied dance of unbridled energy. It is really more than time that pianists should study this remarkable work and add it to their répertoire. When it is better known this Concerto will surely become popular.

The fourth piano Concerto, in C minor, Op. 44, is generally considered the finest of the series. It is divided into two parts comprising five changes of *tempo*. The composer has constructed this work mainly on two themes, which undergo various processes of metamorphosis and express a corresponding number of emotions. In this Concerto, as well as in all his other works, Saint-Saëns never loses the thread of his discourse. He knows full well what he intends to say, and expresses himself in a clear, lucid manner.

The curious theme heard at the beginning has a sharp, incisive character which suggests an inquiry and is easily recognizable throughout. The second most important theme first appears in the form of a chorale played by the wood wind instruments. The psychological impression conveyed by the whole first movement seems to be that of an anxious striving after some ideal, with moments of doubt followed by resignation.

With the second movement a spirit of energy supervenes: confidence has been restored. The music assumes various fantastic forms, and the solo instrument is kept very busy. The appearance of a tune with an irresistible amount of " go " disposes of any remnants of pessimism, and the final appearance of theme number two, first heard as a chorale in the opening movement, but now converted into a joyful expression of optimism, brings the Concerto to a brilliant and triumphant conclusion.

Originally produced on October 31, 1875, in Paris, at one of Colonne's concerts, this Concerto was played for the first time in London at a concert given by Mr. W. Ganz on May 24, 1879. Since then it has become well known and universally admired.

The composer's fifth piano Concerto, in F, Op. 104, was written much later, in the winter of 1896. It differs in several ways from the others. Composed during, or under the impression of, a sojourn in Egypt, it reflects the calm and reposeful beauty of the Nile and evokes the varied aspects of life in those favoured regions. There is here no feeling of pessimism or of striving after the unrealizable. A debonair attitude, possibly due to life under sunny skies, takes its place. The music becomes frankly Oriental in the Andante and includes a reminiscence of a ditty sung by the boatmen on the Nile. In the Finale, Saint-Saëns has sought to describe his experiences on the sea voyage.

A note of realism is introduced by the suggestion of the sound of the propeller, while the serenity of the voyage is interrupted by a short storm.   Altogether, the Concerto is an interesting and picturesque work.

The Fantasia entitled *Africa,* also for piano and orchestra, is founded on themes indigenous to the Black Continent.   It was written in 1891 and is a very effective concert piece, which the much-regretted Raoul Pugno used to play to perfection.   The hot African sun shines throughout on this bright composition, the last portion of which is brimful of the wildest *entrain.*

The *Rapsodie d'Auvergne,* Op. 73, and the *Allegro Appassionato,* Op. 70, are less-known works also written for piano and orchestra.

The first of the three violin Concertos written by Saint-Saëns belongs to the early days of his career and was composed in 1859.   It is labelled Op. 17, and was preceded by the second, written a year before, but not published until twenty years later, and bearing the *opus* number 58.   These two Concertos have not enjoyed the same vogue as the third, in B minor, Op. 61, which has long since become a prime favourite with violinists. The popularity obtained by this last work is not surprising, for besides offering the violinist every opportunity for the exhibition of his skill it has qualities that render it attractive to the cultured musician.   It is more than mere virtuoso music and, if not unduly profound, is poetically conceived and abounds in piquant and novel devices pleasing to the ear.   Its three movements, the second a graceful barcarolle quite Italian in colour, at the end of which a charming effect is produced by the employment of harmonics for the solo instrument, are all interesting and effective.

Other works for violin and orchestra which merit attention are the well-known *Introduction et Rondo Capriccioso*, Op. 28, written in 1863, which is in the répertoire of all violinists and has become universally and justly popular; an excellent so-called Concert Piece, Op. 62, composed in 1880; a *Havanaise*, Op. 83, and a *Caprice Andalous*, Op. 122, two characteristic examples of the composer's exoticism.

The master has also contributed two works to the meagre list of concertos for violoncello. The first of these, in A minor, Op. 33, is a wholly delightful and very individual work which has met with pronounced success. Short and compact in form, it consists of only one movement composed of three sections, and it might well be prefixed by the motto *multum in parvo*. The centre portion takes the form of a most fascinating little minuet played by the muted strings, the violoncello entering with captivating effect. Detached from its surroundings, this section has often been played as a short solo, notably by the famous violoncellist Joseph Hollman. Saint-Saëns has written a second violoncello Concerto, in D minor, Op. 119, composed in 1902, an interesting work which has not become so well known as the first. The list of his compositions for solo instruments with orchestra further includes a Tarantella for Flute and Clarinet, Op. 6; a Romance for Horn, Op. 36; and a Romance for Flute, Op. 37.

CHAPTER V

CHAMBER MUSIC

IF Saint-Saëns shines as a composer for the orchestra, he appears to equal advantage in the more restricted domain of Chamber music. It may be said with truth that he was the first French composer who showed himself able to compete successfully in this more intimate yet supremely difficult *genre* with the German masters of the past. A Sonata, a Trio, or a Quartet exhibits the technical qualifications of a musician as much as anything. It is difficult here to slur over defects of form or to produce an effect by meretricious means.

The natural bent of Saint-Saëns, his upbringing and early knowledge of the classics, imperatively pointed to his expressing himself through the same medium as those great masters with whom he had lived on such familiar terms since the days of his childhood. Consequently it is not surprising that, amid the strenuous activities of his life, the enormous labours implied by combining the careers of composer and executant, he should from time to time have enriched the répertoire of Chamber music with works in which he could express himself independently and untrammelled by any outward considerations.

It is notable that in these works he should have asserted his individuality in so pronounced a manner, while at the same time not departing too much from those traditional forms gradually evolved by his predecessors.

His first important contribution to what is known as Chamber music, a Quintet for pianoforte and strings, Op. 14, was composed in 1855 and published some ten years later. As an example of the composer's skill, even at so early a period of his life, the Quintet is full of interest. There is nothing in the music which suggests the work of a neophyte. Classical in style, there are moments when it seems to anticipate the later Saint-Saëns—for instance, in the nervous accents of the vertiginous Presto. The sanity, clearness of expression, intuitive feeling for form, so characteristic of the composer, are present in this work, which forms a remarkable prelude to his other labours in the same field.

The personality of Saint-Saëns reveals itself thoroughly in the Trio, No. 1, in F, Op. 18, composed in 1863, which is one of the best known and most generally popular works of its kind. It is said to have been thought out during the course of a trip in the Pyrenees, and this is borne out by the character of the music, the evident outcome of youthful spontaneity, suggesting the light-heartedness of one who has for the time being thrown cares to the wind and whose inspiration has been stimulated by the wonders of nature.

Blithely does the first movement commence, and one can well imagine the young traveller eagerly starting on his journey. The opening theme has a pleasant, easy swing about it, and the impression it creates is never allowed to weaken. It is succeeded by an Andante of surprising originality and beauty, which opens slowly and gravely in the key of A minor, a solemn theme being played in octaves by the piano, while the violin sounds the A as an upper pedal note. One can imagine a procession of mediæval monks passing through the cloisters of an old monastery. A lovely episode in the major furnishes a charming contrast to the preceding solemnity. The Scherzo brings us once more into the brightest sunlight and amid scenes of light and joy, conditions which are further amplified in the Finale. Truly a most delightful work without one dull moment, one which can be heard again and again with profit and pleasure.

If a spirit of lively optimism prevails in the charming Trio above mentioned, the reverse is the case as regards the Sonata for violoncello, No. 1, in C minor, Op. 32, a veritable masterpiece of strength and concentrated emotion. Written soon after the fateful war of 1870, it seems as if the composer had poured forth all his feelings of anguish into his work. The light-heartedness of his younger days has vanished for the moment. Here all is grave and earnest; even the usual Scherzo is absent. The magnificent first movement, in which the piano and violoncello strive for ascendancy one against the other, is superbly worked out without departing appreciably from recognised forms. This is succeeded by a strikingly impressive Andante founded on a chorale of somewhat severe character, while a Finale teeming with energy brings this very remarkable composition to a close.

Somewhat tempered in spirit, but possessing a certain affinity with the above Sonata, is the well-known Quartet

in B flat, Op. 41, for pianoforte, violin, viola, and
violoncello, which dates from the year 1875. The
same mastery of resource, nobility of thought, perfection of detail, may be found here. The feeling of revolt
against fate, expressed in the Sonata, has given way
here to a more settled attitude of mind, and the work
exhibits the composer in two opposite and essentially
characteristic moods.

The first movement suggests a placid feeling of contentment, the opening passage for violin and viola
being vaguely reminiscent of a theme in the first violin
sonata of Rubinstein. A pleasing current of melody
permeates the entire movement. In the Andante
maestoso we find Saint-Saëns in a more serious and
scholastic mood. One feels instinctively that the music
must be played in very strict time. It starts with a
rhythmical figure, which is afterwards employed in
conjunction with a chorale, the two blending admirably
together. This Andante deserves close attention and
study. It is succeeded by what stands for the Scherzo,
although not so termed, and here we find the composer
in his most freakish mood, as in the *Danse Macabre*.
The strains are weirdly humorous and might appropriately describe the nocturnal capers of sprites. The
Finale, vigorous and straightforward, is again frankly
classical in structure and admirably developed, allusions
to two themes from the first movement contributing
to impart a sense of unity to the Quartet.

A work of an entirely different style is the Septet,
in E flat, Op. 65, for trumpet, pianoforte, two violins,
viola, violoncello, and double bass. Apart from being
in the same key, it has nothing in common with the
famous Septet of Beethoven. The introduction of a

trumpet into a work of this kind is explained by the fact that the Septet was written for a musical society in Paris known as *La Trompette*, where pleasant reunions took place at stated times. Saint-Saëns, naturally, was ever welcome at these informal concerts, and, in order to mark his appreciation of their value, he undertook to compose a work specially for one of these occasions. So that there might be no doubt concerning its association with the society in question, he did not hesitate to introduce so unusual an instrument as the trumpet into the scheme of his work. The Septet is conceived after the manner of the old Suites, and the composer was evidently in an archaic frame of mind when he wrote it. It includes a Preambule, a Minuet, an Andante, a Gavotte, and a Finale, all eminently attractive, simple in structure, and generally more suggestive of the eighteenth than of the nineteenth century, the whole being a highly pleasing evocation of a period artistic and refined in spite of its formality.

It may be mentioned that it was at a concert of the above-named society, *La Trompette*, that Saint-Saëns produced his humorous Fantasia entitled *Le Carnaval des animaux*. The only piece from this work which has appeared in print is the exquisite melody known as " Le Cygne," played everywhere either as a violin or 'cello solo. This delicate and refined inspiration stands out in contrast to the other parts of a work in which the elephant is represented by a solo on the double bass, and in which figure donkeys, antediluvian animals, and, supreme irony, a virtuoso pianist ! A performance of this work, written in a moment of joyous humour, would surely be welcome and afford an antidote to the dullness that so often prevails in concert-rooms.

Saint-Saëns has written two violin sonatas. The first and best known one, composed in 1885, is in D minor and labelled Op. 75. Adopting the same plan as in the fourth piano Concerto and the Symphony in C minor, the composer has divided his work into two parts, connecting the first two movements together and doing the same thing as regards the two last. The hand that penned the Quartet is easily recognized in this very attractive Sonata written in an evident spirit of contentment. There is nothing in the music calculated to tear at the heart-strings. On the contrary, it induces a pleasurable feeling of satisfaction due to its melodic character and smooth musical treatment. What, for example, can be more piquant than the graceful theme of the Allegretto in G minor, and how well does this same theme sound when employed later on in conjunction with a fluently melodious passage allotted to the violin! In the Finale, which runs a merry course after the style of a *moto perpetuo*, there reoccurs a charming motive, very typical of the composer, which figured in the first movement. Altogether the work is a genial and highly attractive example of the modern sonata, a fact which violinists have not been slow in recognizing.

The second Trio for pianoforte, violin, and violoncello, in E minor, Op. 92, composed in 1892, counts among the composer's best works in the domain of Chamber music. It is modern in spirit, though classical in form, and contains various innovations of the highest interest to the musician. One can readily realize that the composition of this work must have been a labour of love.

The second Sonata for violin, in E flat, Op. 102, was

composed in 1896, and also deserves attention. Unfortunately the limited space at my disposal does not permit of more than a passing allusion to this and other works of the composer whose output is so enormous that several volumes would be required to do ample justice to it. It will, therefore, be necessary to be content with a bare mention of the very interesting and poetical String Quartet, Op. 112, composed in 1899.

Brief mention must also be made of the second Sonata for violoncello, in F, Op. 123, which includes an elaborate set of Variations. The composer has always shown a partiality for this beautiful instrument, for which he wrote one of his earliest Chamber works, a Suite, Op. 16, composed in 1862, consisting of five parts and including a charmingly quaint Serenade. The list of his compositions further contains several works of smaller dimensions, which have found acceptance in many a drawing-room. Enough, though, has been said to give an idea of the importance of the master's contributions to the more serious forms of Chamber music.

If we turn to the works written by Saint-Saëns for piano solo it is to find that his output in this direction is, comparatively speaking, small. He has preferred to devote himself to elaborating works of larger proportions and to employ the piano in conjunction with the orchestra.

The set of Six Etudes, Op. 52, composed in 1877, deserves the first mention. These studies are well known, and one of them, the " Etude en forme de Valse," has been played by most professional pianists. Admirable on account of their technical value, they also

8

possess real intrinsic musical qualities. It cannot be
averred that they are easy to play, the " Etude de rythme "
being concerned with the combination of two notes
against three. Two of the studies are fugues written
in a severe scholastic style. A second set of twelve
studies, Op. 111, appeared in 1899, and should prove
of great value to advanced students of the piano. Three
mazurkas, one of which in G minor is particularly
attractive, must not be forgotten. An excellent concert
piece is the " Menuet et Valse," Op. 56, composed in
1878. In this the composer has very cleverly joined a
minuet of classical style to a brilliant modern waltz.
A *Piano Album*, Op. 72, containing six pieces, and a
Suite of four pieces in the olden style, Op. 90, also
deserve mention.

Besides the above original compositions for the piano
Saint-Saëns has written quite a large number of excellent
transcriptions and arrangements of works by other
composers. Notable among these are two admirable
sets of pieces transcribed from Bach, and the well-known
Caprice on ballet airs from Gluck's *Alceste*.

A work which stands apart is the famous set of
Variations for two pianos on a theme of Beethoven,
which is a veritable masterpiece. The theme in question
is the trio of the Minuet in Beethoven's piano Sonata,
Op. 31. This simple theme has been treated in a
masterly manner by Saint-Saëns, who presents it under
various transformations, yet never loses what might be
termed its main outline.

Other interesting works for two pianos are the
Scherzo, Op. 87, a wildly exhilarating and fanciful
composition, a Polonaise, Op. 77, Caprice Arabe, Op.
86, and Caprice Héroïque, Op. 106.

CHAPTER VI

MASSES, ORATORIOS, CANTATAS (SACRED AND SECULAR), ETC.

HAVING attempted to give an idea of the work achieved by Saint-Saëns in the fields of Opera, Symphony, and Chamber music, there still remain for consideration the various choral compositions for church and concert-room. These are by no means negligible either in quality or quantity. The prize Ode to Saint Cecilia, written by him while still in his teens, has never been published, so we cannot tell in what manner he sung the praises of the patroness of Music.

A *Messe Solennelle* for four voices, with chorus, orchestra, and organ, was composed in 1856 and published the following year. As this is the composer's only published setting of the words of the *Mass*, it is presumably the one which called forth the following highly appreciative expression of opinion from no less a judge than Liszt. In a long letter to Saint-Saëns, written from Rome on July 19, 1869, acknowledging the reception of various compositions, Liszt writes: " Let us speak first of the *Mass* : this is a capital, grand, beautiful, admirable work—so good that, among contemporary works of the same kind, I know perhaps of none so striking by the elevation of the sentiment, the religious character, the sustained, adequate, vigorous style and consummate mastery. It is like a magnificent Gothic cathedral in which Bach would conduct his orchestra ! ''

This is already pretty high praise, but Liszt does not stop here. After making some practical suggestions with regard to the performance of the *Mass* in church, he proceeds : " You will find these small matters carefully noted down on your score, which I will venture to return to you, begging you to let me have it back again soon, for I must possess this extraordinary work, which has its place between Bach and Beethoven."

The value of this praise is immensely enhanced when we remember that it emanated from the composer of the admirable *Mass* written for the consecration of the Basilica at Gran, from one whose knowledge of music was as unrivalled as the broadness of his views, from the untiring and unselfish champion of Wagner and of every musician of genius, from one who thought more of others than he did of himself, from Franz Liszt, the great, the generous, the unapproachable artist ! We know that it was owing to the encouragement of Liszt that Saint-Saëns completed his *Samson and Delilah*, and that this beautiful Biblical opera was performed for the first time.

Having composed one setting of the *Mass*, Saint-Saëns has not followed the example of so many other composers who have provided several versions of the sacred text. Later on in his career, in 1878, he wrote a *Requiem Mass*, Op. 54, and is said to have taken only eight days to do it !

The text of the Mass for the Dead is susceptible of

various musical interpretations and has attracted many composers, notably Mozart, Cherubini, Berlioz, Schumann, Verdi, Dræsecke, Dvoràk, Fauré, Bruneau, Stanford. The poignancy of the words and their tragic signification irresistibly call for musical expression. The great difficulty in so doing is to steer clear of bombastic and theatrical effects while realizing as far as possible the sense and solemnity of the text. The crux invariably occurs in the *Dies Iræ* and particularly in the setting of the *Tuba Mirum.*

To succeed in bringing to the mind the realization of the trumpets of the Last Judgment is no easy matter. Berlioz, in his *Requiem,* for this purpose employed an enormous orchestra and multiplied the number of brass instruments, endeavouring in this way to induce a feeling of awe and consternation. He directed in the full score of his work that " four small orchestras of brass instruments should be placed isolatedly at the four corners of the great choral and instrumental body, the horns alone remaining in the middle of the large orchestra."

Verdi, in his beautiful *Requiem,* is more moderate than Berlioz, and his setting of the *Dies Iræ* is wonderfully impressive and dramatic. Alfred Bruneau, who has also written a *Requiem,* has treated this portion of the text in a very original and striking manner, trumpets placed on the right and left sides of the orchestra alternately sounding the notes of the fine old liturgical chant usually employed in connection with the Office for the Departed.

Saint-Saëns has avoided anything approaching to sensationalism in his setting, which is intensely devotional in style. The words are interpreted with a becoming

gravity of expression, while the whole work moves on
an elevated plane below which it never falls.   If one felt
inclined to single out any special section it would be
the *Agnus Dei*, the effect of which is most touching.
Particularly admirable is the manner in which the work
concludes, the gradual diminution of tone, the voices
in a whispered prayer appealing for consolation, the
music finally dying away in an almost inaudible *pianissimo*.

A work of great charm belonging to the early career
of Saint-Saëns is the so-called *Oratorio de Noël*, Op. 12,
for soli and chorus, with accompaniment of a quintet
of strings, harp, and organ.   This was written in 1858,
the year of the composer's appointment as organist of
the Madeleine.   It is divided into nine numbers, the
words being versicles selected from the Office of the
Day and the Midnight Mass.   Simple in structure and
melodious in style, it conveys the feeling of joyful hope
associated with the occasion.   The opening Allegretto
Pastorale, conceived in the right spirit, is a charming
and soothing little movement.   To be specially mentioned are : the solo for mezzo-soprano, " Expectans ";
the " Benedictus," for soprano and baritone ;   and
particularly, the really beautiful trio for soprano, tenor,
and baritone, " Tecum presidium."   This Christmas
Oratorio appeals to one especially by reason of its
melodic grace, simplicity, and finish.   There is here no
attempt to indulge in over-elaboration, yet the music
fulfils its purpose in the most adequate manner, which
is all that can be desired.

Another work which commands attention is the
setting for soli, chorus, and orchestra of *Psalm XVIII.*,
Cœli enarrant, Op. 42.   Written some years later, it
exemplifies the more serious and scholastic side of the

composer's nature, besides displaying those imaginative
qualities which are rarely absent from his works. The
words of the Psalm, one of the most beautiful of all,
celebrate the glory of God and breathe a spirit of thank-
fulness and humility. In setting them to music Saint-
Saëns has not been content with demonstrating his
ability in contrapuntal technicalities, but has endeavoured
with success to express their meaning in sounds. The
general impression conveyed by this fine Psalm is one
of confident optimism. It is a work which should not
be neglected by our Choral Societies. An uncommon
feature is the presence of a Quartet for four baritones.
It is said that at the time when the work was written
there happened to be several good baritones among
the choristers of the Madeleine, which accounts for
the unusual grouping of voices.

The Oratorio is a form of musical art which has
never appealed to the French in the same manner as
it has to us. Many reasons could be adduced to explain
this fact. In France composers have been generally
attracted by the stage and have concentrated their
efforts in this direction. Still, from time to time,
there have appeared choral works, sacred or secular,
which have attracted attention and proved that French
composers could be equally at home whether in church,
concert-room, or theatre.

Berlioz half ruined himself in the expenses incurred
by the production of his *Damnation de Faust,* and later
on wrote his *L'Enfance du Christ.* Félicien David made
his reputation with *Le Désert,* the first attempt to
introduce a definite Oriental colour into the music of
France. After the war of 1870 composers turned more
towards the Oratorio or Cantata. Massenet obtained

his first success with *Marie Magdeleine*, and followed
this up with *Eve* and *La Vierge*. In the meanwhile
César Franck was slowly elaborating his vast setting of
The Beatitudes.

Saint-Saëns seemed specially designed to succeed in
a *genre* which afforded such ample scope for the display
of his talent. So it came to pass that in 1875, at the
period when he was busy writing Symphonic Poems,
Concertos, and other works, he found time to devote
to the composition of an Oratorio, *Le Déluge*, which
some consider one of his best works. I am not aware
whether this has ever been performed in London.
At any rate the Prelude is extremely well known, and
is one of the most universally popular pieces of Saint-
Saëns, of the dual nature of whose style it affords an
admirable example. It commences in a severe and
austere manner, somewhat like Bach. After a few
introductory bars, a theme of an expressive and melancholy nature is treated fugally, and gradually leads
to a melody of great charm played by a solo violin
and very softly accompanied by the strings. The
chords at the close are a little suggestive of Gounod.
This beautiful Prelude, remarkable for its simplicity
and feeling, in a way presents a synthesis of the entire
work, which was suggested by the passage in Genesis
" And God repented having created the world." The
solemnity of the opening chords, the mystic feeling
conveyed by the fugal section, accord well with the
gravity of the subject, while the lovely melody which
follows is meant to suggest humanity in its original
state of purity.

The work is divided into three parts and is constructed
in a very original manner, the contrasts being admirably

devised. The very fact of prefixing a work on such a subject by a Prelude of so quiet, one might say intimate, a character evinced an intention to avoid beaten tracks. In the *Deluge* Saint-Saëns has been faithful to the same methods he has employed in his operas and shown the same independence, alternately adopting scholastic devices or resorting to modern methods. For instance, the Oratorio includes no fewer than three fugues. The first portion of the work is scored for strings only, the composer having reserved the full force of the orchestra for the second portion, which contains a symphonic description of the flood. The difficulty of suggesting so mighty a cataclysm of nature without relying on mere dynamical effects of sound was obvious, but the composer not only succeeded in avoiding any suspicion of meretriciousness, but in painting a strikingly effective symphonic tableau representing the rise and overflowing of the waters. For this purpose Saint-Saëns adopted a contrary plan to the one he had followed in the first part of his work, where he had restricted himself to the employment of strings, for he not only made use of the full orchestra, but strengthened it by the addition of two more trombones, making five altogether, and four low saxhorns. The Oratorio is planned for two solo voices and chorus. It counts among the master's best works, and the fact that it should be persistently neglected in London, especially after the triumphant success of *Samson and Delilah*, is one of the many inexplicable matters that abound in our musical life.

If we have neglected the *Deluge*, we have still less excuse in having allowed so interesting a work as *The Lyre and the Harp* to remain on the shelf, considering that its original production took place in England, at the Birmingham Festival of 1879. This Cantata is a musical setting of Victor Hugo's *Ode*, the English version being from the pens of Sydney Samuel and James Donzel. It was favourably received at the time, the solo parts being sung by Mmes Lemmens Sherrington and Patey, Messrs. Cummings and Santley.

The idea permeating Victor Hugo's *Ode* is concerned with the contrasts between the Pagan and Christian ideals, as exemplified in the poetry of antiquity, singing of sensuality, and that of modern times, inspired by the principles of Christian charity : the Lyre representing the one, and the Harp the other, sing alternately in order to influence the poet.

Instead of being written in the form of a duet, as the poem would appear to suggest, the Cantata has been divided into various sections, solos, duets, choruses, and so on. This plan imparts rather a formal aspect to the work as a whole, though it offers scope for diversity of treatment. As usual, the composer has known how to combine the colours on his musical palette in a variety of tones, and the work, which was greatly admired by Liszt, is one which should certainly be revived.

A long lapse of years was destined to intervene between the production of this interesting and poetical Cantata and that of the next choral work of importance to be produced in England. During these years the reputation of Saint-Saëns, already very great, had steadily advanced, and he had been universally recognized as the foremost living French composer as well as one of the great masters of the age.

The work in question, entitled *The Promised Land,*

was described as " a short Oratorio, for soli, chorus, and orchestra," the words being arranged from the Scriptures by Hermann Klein. It was produced for the first time at the Gloucester Musical Festival of 1813. In a note prefixed to the score, Mr. Hermann Klein wrote that " among the old Jewish legends not to be found in the Bible, there are several that are intended to explain why Moses was not permitted to enter the ' Promised Land.' They are extremely picturesque, but not altogether convincing." He further says that " a modern interpretation of the Biblical words puts it that ' Moses and Aaron were not permitted to enter the Promised Land because they did not have the proper confidence in God in calling water from the rock.' Such is the interpretation of the Mosaic narrative that has been adopted in the present instance." Mr. Klein added that the text of the Oratorio had been taken entirely from the Books of Numbers and Deuteronomy, and from the Psalms.

In this Oratorio Saint-Saëns has not made any attempt to break fresh ground, and the simplicity and formal nature of the music caused a certain amount of surprise when the work was produced. The composer has been content here to keep to the old traditional forms, and has divided his work into solos, duets, choruses, joined together by recitatives. His own individuality, how-ever, asserts itself now and again, and the work deserved to be reckoned higher than it was at the time of its production. It is strictly and evidently purposely conceived in a classical style suggestive of Bach and Handel, though modern harmonies and modulations are not absent. Still, these square-cut choruses, though effective enough, seem to belong to a past epoch. In

one instance the chorus, unaccompanied, after singing
a hymn, break out into veritably Handelian roulades,
introduced possibly in deference to the supposed
partiality of English audiences for such things. Of
course, all this is admirably wrought, as might be expected, but it is more satisfactory to meet the composer
when not wearing an eighteenth-century peruke. This
we do at the beginning of the second part, in the duet
between Moses and Aaron, with its quaint figuration
in the accompaniment and simple vocal accents. Here
and there picturesque details are also noticeable, and
the recitatives are broadly and effectively written.

The most important choral works of Saint-Saëns
having been mentioned, it will be necessary to be brief
regarding other compositions coming under the above
category, such as *Les Noces de Prométhée*, the Cantata
which won a prize in 1867, and *Nuit Persane*, a Cantata
for soli, chorus, and orchestra, founded on the very
characteristic and picturesque set of six songs entitled
Mélodies Persanes. He has also composed quite a large
number of choruses for different voices, as well as many
settings of sacred words.

As a song-writer Saint-Saëns occupies a distinguished
place among contemporary French composers. Particular attention should be drawn to his strikingly
dramatic and vividly emotional setting for mezzo-
soprano and orchestra of Victor Hugo's ballade *La
Fiancée du Timbalier*, which is well known.

CHAPTER VII

LITERARY WORKS

OPINIONS ON MUSIC AND MUSICIANS

THE enormous musical productivity of Saint-Saëns, evidenced by the number and importance of his works, would lead one to suppose that he would have had little leisure left to devote to other matters, particularly if one takes into account that, in addition to the time occupied in attending to his duties as organist during the early years of his career, he had acquired great fame as a pianist and was necessarily obliged to lead the feverish life of an executant, travelling hither and thither without much rest. Yet he has found it possible also to enter the literary arena, to distinguish himself not only as a musical critic, but as a writer on other subjects.

All who have enjoyed the privilege of meeting this extraordinary man cannot fail to have been struck by the brilliancy of his conversational powers, the flashes of wit that illumine his remarks, the great breadth of his views, and the variety of his tastes. These traits are all present in his writings, which are never laboured, stilted, or artificial. One feels instinctively that as he thinks, so he writes, true to himself and absolutely in-

different as to whether his opinions correspond with
the ideas prevalent at the moment. This sincerity
and independence of thought are very refreshing and
none too common qualities.

Deeply interested in anything partaking to his art,
and eager to express his opinions and discuss or combat
those of others, Saint-Saëns has often been seized with
the *cacoëthes scribendi,* to the great delight of his readers
and admirers, who, whether or not they have been
able to agree with what he said, cannot have failed to
be impressed by the cogency of his arguments and
captivated by the easy flow of his language.

Like so many other French composers, Saint-Saëns
has wielded the pen of the critic and has contributed
to several newspapers. Various articles of his have been
collected and reproduced in separate volumes. The
first of these appeared in 1885 under the title of *Harmonie
et Mélodie.* The date is important, as some of the
articles bear upon questions which were at that time
much discussed. One of these was the Wagner question,
which had then reached a curious phase in Paris.

Apart from the famous and ill-fated production of
Tannhäuser at the Opéra in 1861, and a few performances
of *Rienzi* at the Théâtre Lyrique in 1869, no stage
representations of Wagner's operas had been given in
Paris, though extracts from his works had been frequently
performed in the concert-room, where they had met
with a very mixed reception. Conscious of Wagner's
immense genius, Saint-Saëns had strenuously taken his
part at a moment when there was a certain risk in so
doing. As time went on, a different spirit began to
prevail, and indiscriminate adoration gradually took the
place of ignorant abuse. Then it was that Saint-Saëns

thought it necessary to state his ideas plainly on the subject.

The introduction to *Harmonie et Mélodie* contains what may be taken as the writer's profession of musical faith. Answering the accusation that he is denying Wagner after having profited by him, he says : " Not only do I not deny him, but I glory in having studied him and profited by him, as it was my right and my duty. I have done the same as regards Sebastian Bach, Haydn, Beethoven, Mozart, and all the masters of all the schools. I do not on that account consider myself obliged to say of each one of them that he alone is god and that I am his prophet. In reality, it is neither Bach, nor Beethoven, nor Wagner whom I love ; it is art. I am an eclectic. This is perhaps a great defect, but it is impossible for me to correct it : one cannot alter one's nature. Again, I love liberty passionately, and cannot bear to have admirations imposed upon me. Enthusiasms to order (*les enthousiasmes de commande*) freeze the blood in my veins, and render me incapable of appreciating the most beautiful works."

In order to give an adequate idea of the value of this volume it would be necessary to quote to a greater extent than it is possible to do. The subjects discussed are treated so lightly and yet so surely and logically that they are rendered absorbingly interesting.

In the first chapter the author discusses the relative importance of harmony and melody, exposing the ignorant and futile ideas of those people who consider that music is composed of those two elements, that " harmony, the secondary element, proceeds from melody ; that melody is spontaneously conceived and is the outcome of genius, whereas harmony is the

product of calculation and science." This article, written
in 1879, was aimed at the devotees of the older forms
of Italian opera.

In the next chapter we have a very interesting account
of the first Bayreuth Festival in 1876 and the impressions produced on Saint-Saëns by Wagner's great trilogy
or, as he terms it, tetralogy. That this impression was
very great stands to reason, but this did not prevent
him from making various criticisms which are in the
main perfectly just and reasonable. Certain culminating points in the four music dramas called forth his
enthusiastic admiration, such as the great scene between
Siegmund and Sieglinde in the first act of the *Walküre*,
concerning which he wrote : " Here is indeed the
theatre of the future ; neither opera nor non-lyrical
drama will ever produce such an emotion in one's
soul." *Siegfried* also aroused his admiration, and he
said that " from the heights of the last act of *Götterdämmerung*, the entire work appears in its almost supernatural immensity, like the chain of the Alps seen from
the summit of Mont Blanc."

The following opinion concerning Schumann, written
in 1879, is worth quoting : " Schumann is not the man
for long-winded compositions, and one must always
expect to find weak parts in those of his works which
are of vast proportions ; only *Manfred* maintains itself
throughout. A sort of musical Alfred de Musset,
Schumann is the man of exquisite things : he knows
how to be great in small styles and in small frameworks.
Incapable of writing a work like *Elijah*, he has thoroughly
beaten Mendelssohn in the *lied* and in piano music.
For those who know the ' Forest Scenes ' and the
' Kreisleriana,' the celebrated ' Songs without Words '

are only like shadows.   Where Mendelssohn painted aquarelles, Schumann has engraved cameos."

Saint-Saëns' admiration for Liszt has already been mentioned in a former chapter.   In the present volume he devotes an article to this master's Symphonic Poems. He also has something to say about Offenbach, to whose productivity and melodic gifts he renders justice, drawing attention to the extraordinary facility and rapidity of execution which characterized the composer of *Orphée aux Enfers*, saying that " he literally improvized and in writing his scores he had a system of abbreviation which he pushed to the last limits."

In dipping into this fascinating volume it would be easy to extract a quantity of delightful passages and ideas of real value, but there are other volumes to be considered, and to these I must now pass.

Portraits et Souvenirs appeared in 1899 and, as the title suggests, also consists of a collection of articles. These are divided into three sections respectively named Portraits, Souvenirs, and Variétés.   The composers who furnish the subjects of the Portraits are Berlioz, Liszt, Gounod, Massé, and Rubinstein.   Some delightful recollections of Bizet, who was the author's intimate friend, are included in the second section, in which may also be found the charming account of Saint-Saëns' experiences at Cambridge, to which allusion has already been made.   The articles in the last portion are mainly polemical in character and devoted to opinions and discussions concerning various questions relating to musical art, as may be gathered by the following alluring titles : " The Defence of the Opéra-Comique," " Lyrical Drama and Musical Drama," " The Wagnerian Illusion," etc.

9

The general trend of the author's ideas may be gathered by the following sentences at the commencement of the short Preface : " It would seem as if a century had elapsed since the time when I wrote *Harmonie et Mélodie*. ' Harmony,' then, signified science, ' Melody,' inspiration. The situation has turned round ; amateurs who refused to make the smallest effort to understand music have been seized with a passion for the obscure and the incomprehensible. They are irritated or disdainful if the instruments of the orchestra do not run about from one side to the other like poisoned rats ; a simple accompaniment makes them shrug their shoulders." This need not be taken too seriously, but it is an amusing cut at those amateurs whose one object is to appear to be " up to date."

The articles on Berlioz, Liszt, and Gounod deserve to be read carefully. Saint-Saëns knew these three famous men intimately, and admired their works. They, who were considerably his seniors in age, had all three shown the greatest interest in his career and encouraged him to the best of their power. A double feeling of sympathy, therefore, bound him to them.

The following appreciation of Berlioz as a man will be read with interest, as it should serve to modify the current notions regarding the supposed cantankerousness of his disposition : " In addition to my complete admiration, I had for him a strong feeling of affection due to the kindness he had always shown me, and of which I was justly proud, as well as on account of private qualities I had discovered in him, so entirely opposite to the reputation he had in the world, where he passed for being proud, spiteful, and ill-natured. He was, on the contrary, good—good even to weakness—grateful

for the least marks of interest one showed him, and of
an admirable simplicity which gave still more value to
his biting wit and to his sallies, because one never felt
that search for effect, that desire to dazzle people which
often spoils so many good things."

Particularly admirable is the article devoted to Liszt,
from which the following passage is extracted : " Liszt,
like Berlioz, makes *Expression* the aim of instrumental music, devoted by tradition to the exclusive
worship of form and of impersonal beauty. This is
not meant to imply that he has neglected these. Where
could one find purer forms than in the second part of
his *Faust* (Gretchen), in the 'Purgatory' of his *Dante*,
in his *Orpheus* ? But it is by the justness and intensity
of expression that Liszt is really incomparable. His
music speaks, and in order not to hear his word, it is
necessary to stop up one's ears with the plug of fore-
gone conclusion, which is unfortunately always at
hand. It utters the inexpressible." No words could
characterize the music of Liszt better than the above.

Saint-Saëns is equally interesting when writing about
Gounod, whom he knew well, and concerning whom
he gives many highly interesting details, analysing his
principal compositions and pointing out their many
beauties. He entertains a high opinion concerning the
sacred works of the composer of *Faust*, and thinks that
these are more than any others destined to sustain the
glory of his name when time " will have erected him
the golden throne upon which he will receive the incense
of future generations."

A much more recent volume entitled *École Buissonière*
is, like the other two, composed of a selection of articles
published at various times in the columns of news-

papers and magazines. It differs from these, however, inasmuch as whilst they are almost entirely concerned with music and musicians, the present one also deals with a variety of other subjects. Saint-Saëns is a great thinker. He has an insatiable thirst for knowledge and a wonderfully logical mind. Science, astronomy, philosophy, have all attracted him, and he has found time to devote to their study. His style is ever lucid, and he never indulges in tiresome circumlocution, but goes straight to the point. The articles in the present volume are grouped under the following headings : Souvenirs, Voyages, Artistic Questions, Sacred Music, Portraits, Scientific Fantasies, and Varieties.

The first article provides us with fascinating details of the composer's earliest childhood. His marvellous musical gifts met with every encouragement in the home. The initial stages of his musical development would appear to have caused him no trouble, and Gounod was wont to say to him, " You have never had a musical childhood." Yet he must have worked hard and incessantly from his youngest age, for he says that among the vestiges of his childhood are a number of attempts at composition, without counting those he destroyed, airs, choruses, cantatas, symphonies, overtures, which will never appear. He speaks highly of Maleden, his professor of composition, who it appears had a wonderful system of harmony, which he had perfected from that of his master Gottfried Weber. It seems that this method is now taught at the Ecole Niedermeyer, where Saint-Saëns was for a time a professor and where Gabriel Fauré, André Messager, Alexandre Georges, and the organist Gigoux learnt the rudiments of their art.

In the course of the second article Saint-Saëns gives an account of two occasions when, as he says, " he had the honour of being received by Queen Victoria at Windsor Castle." These visits have left an indelible impression on his mind. " Everything has been said about Queen Victoria," he writes, " but one could not praise sufficiently the profound and quite special charm which emanated from her person. She seemed the personification of England ; when she disappeared, the country felt an enormous void, and the splendid personality of King Edward was not too much to fill it."

It is doubtful whether people as a rule realize the enormous difficulties which beset a composer at the outset of his career—difficulties of all sorts, and such that the most famous masters have not succeeded in avoiding, although some have been more fortunate in this respect than others. The composer who aspires to write for the operatic stage finds himself confronted with apparently insuperable obstacles, which require an amount of indomitable spirit, perseverance, and self-confidence to surmount. Many musicians who do not possess these requisites throw up the sponge after making ineffectual struggles, and turn their attention to other work.

In England it is practically hopeless for a native composer to succeed in the operatic field. The French musician is better off, but even in his case it is by no means easy. Anyone who doubts this had better read what Saint-Saëns says in the article entitled " Histoire d'un Opéra-Comique," in which he relates all the tribulations he had to undergo before he was able to have an opera from his pen produced. The work of which he speaks is *Le Timbre d'Argent*, which underwent a variety of transformations before reaching its final shape, and was not performed until the composer was over forty years of age and had acquired universal fame through his instrumental works. Until then, a modest curtain-raiser, *La Princesse Jaune*, was the only work of his which had been given on the stage.

There is so much interesting matter contained in the present volume that one would have to make large quotations in order to render anything like justice to it.

The article on Meyerbeer is particularly worthy of attention. Saint-Saëns protests against the belittling of " the genius of Meyerbeer," which, he says, " is not only an injustice, but an ingratitude." " In all senses," he continues, " conception of the musical drama, treatment of the orchestra, management of the choral masses, *mise en scène* even, he has given us new elements by which our modern works have largely profited." After saying that " his personality is undeniable," that " his style resembles no other," and that " his great admirer and friend Fétis, the celebrated director of the Brussels Conservatoire, insisted with reason on this particularity," Saint-Saëns gives instances of some of the new elements introduced by Meyerbeer into opera : " He has given us, in the place of the long and cumbersome overture, the short and characteristic Prelude, the fortune of which has been so great. To the Preludes of *Robert* and of the *Huguenots* have succeeded those of *Lohengrin*, of *Faust*, of *Tristan*, of *Romeo*, of the *Traviata*, of *Aïda*, and of many others less well known." Further on he continues, " Meyerbeer has given us the sketch, the foretaste of the famous ' leitmotiv ' " ; " he has introduced to the theatre those ensembles of wood instruments so frequent in the grand concertos of Mozart " ;

" he ventured to employ harmonic combinations considered daring at the time " ; " he has developed the
rôle of the cor anglais, which until then had only made
rare and timid appearances, and has introduced the
bass clarinet into the orchestra." The entire article
from which these short extracts are taken is highly
interesting.

Excellent also are the remarks on Rossini, who, as
everyone knows, ceased writing for the stage in 1829,
the year of the production of his *William Tell*, and
spent the remainder of his days in Paris, where he died
in 1868.

Rossini was treated as a sort of a demigod during
the closing years of his life. He used to hold receptions
in the gorgeous apartment he occupied at the corner
of the boulevard and the Chaussée d'Antin, where " the
most brilliant singers and the most illustrious virtuosos "
could be heard. Saint-Saëns was a young man of about
twenty when he was presented to the *maestro*, who
received him very cordially and a month later invited
him to pay him a morning visit. The young musician
naturally hastened to profit by this flattering invitation,
and relates that he found " a very different Rossini to
the evening one, interesting in the highest degree,
with an open mind, with ideas, if not precisely advanced,
at any rate noble and lofty. He gave proof of these
later on when he spoke in favour of the famous *Mass*
of Liszt, exposed when first played at the Church of
Saint Eustache to almost unanimously hostile criticism."
Rossini was evidently a very kind-hearted man, and
showed this at one of his evening receptions when,
there being no programme, he purposely allowed his
guests to think that he was the composer of a piece

by Saint-Saëns for flute and clarinet, which had just
been played, and when these crowded round him
obsequiously with words of admiration on their lips,
he answered quietly that he quite agreed with what
they said, that the duet was not his own composition
but, pointing to Saint-Saëns, who was by his side, that
of " Monsieur, here present."

Among the interesting articles in this volume are
those concerning his trips to Egypt and Algeria. While
approving the various advantages and comforts due to
European civilization, he cannot help feeling that, if a
great deal has been gained thereby, something has also
been lost. " Progress," he writes, " does not mean
amelioration, but progression, that is to say, motion ;
. . . in moving one always leaves something behind,
while one gains other things in front of one, and it
happens often enough that what one has lost was worth
more than what one has gained." Here we have the
artist whose æsthetic sense is shocked by the plain
utilitarian buildings taking the place of " the elegant
and picturesque " structures in the quondam land of
the Pharaohs. He thinks, however, that Pierre Loti
goes too far when he regrets to find railways, steamers,
good hotels, and electric lighting in Egypt, and he
realizes the comfort " in leaving Cairo in the evening,
to go to sleep and awake the next morning in the balmy
temperature of Luxor."

The articles on optical questions and on the planets
will doubtless attract readers who are interested in these
fascinating subjects.

Yet another volume of miscellaneous articles, some
of them quite short, entitled *Au Courant de la Vie*,
appeared soon after the above. It is adorned by a

portrait of the author's charming little griffon dog
called Dalila, who for ten years shared his solitary
existence. Saint-Saëns is extremely fond of the dumb
creation, and this volume includes a very interesting
essay, " Observations d'un ami des bêtes," in which he
analyses with great perspicuity the varying amount of
intelligence possessed by animals and insects. The cat,
according to him, has been infamously calumniated,
and is most faithful when one has been able to win its
good graces, but it does not support bad treatment
and is of a very jealous nature. He gives a curious
instance of a dog who adored hearing the piano and
always came and sat under the pedals, which was very
embarrassing, " but if one wanted him to go, all that
was necessary was to play any piece by Chopin," and
after about eight bars he would leave the room with
his tail between his legs. Saint-Saëns ends this article
by protesting strongly against cruelties towards animals,
and their useless slaughter for no purpose except the
pleasure of killing, also against the abuse of domestic
animals. " It is noticeable," he says, " that the most
fanatical people are the most cruel to animals. . . .
Buddha, in teaching his sectators the doctrine of
metempsychosis, has protected marvellously the animal
which Christianity abandons to all brutalities in pro-
claiming that it is made for man and placing it at his
mercy."

The last article in the present volume is devoted to
a record of the composer's impressions of the United
States. In spite of the fact that he was laid up there
for a while with a severe illness, he seems to have enjoyed
himself, and his remarks show that he was favourably
impressed by the reception he received wherever he

went. " Yes," he says, " America has pleased me, and
I would return there willingly : but is it there that I
would care to live, as the song has it ? Born in the
early half of the nineteenth century, whether I like it
or not, I belong to the past ; in spite of all the comfort
of the young nation, I will always prefer our old towns,
our old relics of the old Continent ! On returning
from New York, Paris struck me as a pretty, elegant
bibelot, but what joy to be back there ! "

In *Problèmes et Mystères,* a booklet published in
1894, the author enters into the regions of philosophy
and metaphysics, and discusses in his usual terse and
lucid manner the eternal questions of the " why, where-
fore, and whither," which have troubled many of us
at one time or another of our lives. I have known this
little work for many years, and have read it over and
over again with ever-renewed pleasure and, I hope,
profit.

The author deals here with controversial subjects,
which he treats in a perfectly fearless spirit, yet in a
manner that could scarcely give offence to any but those
who demur at any discussion whatsoever relating to
matters of belief. The main gist of his argument
resolves itself into a plea in favour of truth and beauty.
He combats both superstition and materialism, and
urges us to labour " so that those who follow us may
be happier than we are, if it be possible, and be grateful
to us for the existence which we have prepared for
them. We will then see that life is good, and, when
the moment arrives, we will close our eyes with the
calm and the satisfaction of the workman who has
finished his task and whose day has been well employed.
The joys offered us by Nature, which she does not refuse

even to the least-favoured amongst us, that which is procured by the discovery of new truths, the æsthetic enjoyment of art, the spectacle of sufferings relieved, and the efforts to suppress them as far as possible—all this may suffice for the happiness of life."

Lofty ideas such as these cannot but meet with approval, and the man who puts them into practice has every chance of finding that happiness and contentment which go with a clear conscience. It would seem preferable to try and do this than to waste time in fruitless endeavours to fathom the unknowable. In this little book Saint-Saëns shows that he not only possesses a clear, logical mind, but also a tender and sympathetic nature.

A booklet of a different type is the one entitled *Germanophilie*. Written in a naturally indignant mood during the worst days of the Great War, it is a strong denunciation of the Teutonic influences the author considers have prevailed in his country. The eternal Wagner question crops up again here. Saint-Saëns divides the French Wagnerites into three categories. The first consists of " the fanatics, for whom Wagner . is the *alpha* and *omega*, who admit of nothing outside his works"; these, he says, are simple maniacs, etc. The second, " the most numerous, who understand nothing of the Wagnerian works, but are taken by the charm of this exciting and troubling music, finding in it an intoxication which M. Frederic Masson has justly compared to that produced by opium." The third category, to which he says that he belongs himself, consisting of those who, " having studied these works, have no illusions concerning their defects (who is free from them ?) and find in their beauties a source of deep æsthetic delights which cannot be met with else-where." The opinion he holds as regards Wagner, it will be noted, has not changed. He has always admired the master's music, but has never allowed his admiration to warp his judgment.

Although this little book was evidently written at a moment when patriotism was very naturally raised to the highest pitch, yet it contains certain well-reasoned expressions of opinion which deserve earnest attention. The author points out the influence of Italian music upon German masters of the past, and says that " this hybridism has made of the music of all these masters a veritably international art, an art of which one might say that it has no country." He considers that " really German music commences with Robert Schumann."

Saint-Saëns does not care much for Brahms, whose works, with a few exceptions, he finds heavy—" of a heaviness that is mistaken for depth of thought." It is interesting to note that Liszt and Tchaikovsky were rather of the same opinion as regards the German com-poser. Liszt held that Raff had more imagination than Brahms, and so did Tchaikovsky. There are frequent references to Brahms in the fascinating *Life and Letters of Tchaikovsky*, translated and edited by Mrs. Rosa Newmarch. The Russian composer found Brahms " cold and obscure, full of pretensions, but without any real depth."

Concerning the present " advanced " musical ten-dencies Saint-Saëns has something to say. " What shocks people to-day will not shock them to-morrow," he writes, " which is equivalent to saying that one can get accustomed to anything. . . . How is it that people will not understand that there are things to which *one must not* become accustomed ? When one has reached the point that one can hear with pleasure, or at any rate with indifference, wrong chords, inexplicable discords, one has become equal to those persons who are not musically organized, having no ear, as people say ; and one has simply proved that here, as elsewhere, extremes meet."

A more recent pamphlet by Saint-Saëns, *Les Idées de M. Vincent d'Indy*, is specially interesting to the musician. It is a critical examination of the *Cours de Composition Musicale*, by Vincent d'Indy. A remark which occurs at the beginning expresses a way of thinking similar to that in the passage quoted above : " Yesterday's dissonance, people say, will be the consonance of to-morrow ; one gets accustomed to everything. But there exist bad habits, and those who get accustomed to crime end badly. . . ." He finds it impossible to consider the disregard of all rules as a progress in the sense that is usually given to the word, and which is the sense of amelioration. " The real sense of the word progress—*progressus*—is march forward, but this does not say to what goal. There is the progress of an illness, which is not an amelioration."

The short extracts I have given from the writings of Saint-Saëns will, I hope, be sufficient to create the wish to peruse these in their entirety and, if possible, in the original language, which gives such a zest to the expression of the author's ideas.

I will conclude by quoting, from the exquisite collection of verses entitled *Rimes familières*, a beautiful sonnet dedicated to a friend, in which Saint-Saëns expresses in poetical language his disagreement with the well-known saying, " Out of sight, out of mind " :

"Non, *loin des yeux* n'est pas *loin du cœur !* le contraire
Pour les âmes d'élite est plutôt vérité.
Quand d'amis sérieux il s'est fait une paire,
L'un ne trahit pas l'autre après l'avoir quitté.

L'éloignement détruit l'amitié du Vulgaire
Pour qui coule toujours l'eau du fleuve Léthé ;
C'est un sable mouvant : Bien fol et téméraire
Qui se fierait jamais a sa solidité !

A nous qui caressons la divine chimère
Et dont les hauts pensers se rencontrent aux cieux,
Que font en plus, en moins, quelques pas sur la terre ?

Loin de l'Antiquité, nous adorons ses dieux,
Nous chérissons Virgile et vénérons Homère ;
Désirant nous revoir nous nous aimerons mieux."

LIST OF COMPOSITIONS

The works mentioned below are published by Messrs. Durand, 4 Place de la Madeleine, except when otherwise stated.

It will be noticed that several of the most important compositions have no Opus numbers.

OPERAS

La Princesse Jaune. Opéra-comique. 1 acte. (1872.) Op. 30.

Le Timbre d'Argent. Drame lyrique. 4 actes. (1877.) Published by Choudens.

Samson et Dalila. Opéra. 3 actes. (1877.) Op. 47.

Étienne Marcel. Opéra. 4 actes. (1879.)

Henry VIII. Opéra. 4 actes. (1883.)

Proserpine. Drame lyrique. (1887.)

Ascanio. Opéra. 5 actes. (1890.)

Phryné. Opéra-comique. 2 actes. (1893.)

Frédégonde. Drame lyrique. 5 actes. (1895), left unfinished by Guiraud and completed by Saint-Saëns. Published by Société d'Edition, Paris.

Les Barbares. Tragédie lyrique. 3 actes et un Prologue. (1901.)

Hélène. Poème lyrique. 1 acte. (1904.)

L'Ancêtre. Drame lyrique. 3 actes. (1906.)

Déjanire. Tragédie lyrique. 4 actes. (1911.)

BALLET

Javotte. Ballet. 1 acte et 3 tableaux. (1896.)

SCENIC MUSIC

Music for Louis Gallet's tragedy, *Déjanire.* (1898.)

,,　　Mme Jane Dieulafoy's drama *Parysatis.* (1902.)

Music for Paul Meurice and A. Vacquerie's tragedy, *Antigone*, after Sophocles. (1894.)

" Racine's tragedy, *Andromaque*. (1903.)

" Henri Lavedan's *L'assassinat du Duc de Guise*. Tableaux d'histoire. (1908.) Op. 128.

" Mme Henri Ferrare's poème antique " La fille du tourneur d'ivoire," d'après une nouvelle de Mme Jean Bertheroy. (1909.) Unpublished.

" " La Foi," trois tableaux symphoniques d'après le drame d'Eugène Brieux. (1910.) Op. 130.

ORATORIOS AND CANTATAS, ETC.

Ode à Sainte Cécile. (1852.) Unpublished.

Scène d'Horace. (P. Corneille.) Soprano, baritone, and orchestra. (1860.) Op. 10.

Les Noces de Prométhée. Cantata. Solo, chorus, and orchestra. (1867.) Published by Hamelle. Op. 19. Words by Romain Cornut.

Cantate. For the centenary of the birth of Hoche. (1868.) Unpublished.

Le Déluge. Poème Biblique en 3 parties. Soli, chorus, and orchestra. (1875.) Op. 45. Words by Louis Gallet.

La Lyre et la Harpe. (Victor Hugo.) Ode for soli, chorus, and orchestra. (1879.) Op. 57.

Nuit Persane. Soli, chorus, and orchestra. Words by Armand Renaud. (1891.)

La Fiancée du Timbalier. (Victor Hugo.) Ballade for mezzo-soprano and orchestra. (1887.) Op. 82.

Pallas Athéné. Soprano and orchestra. Words by J. L. Croze. (1894.)

Lever de soleil sur le Nil. Contralto and orchestra. Words by C. Saint-Saëns. (1898.)

La Nuit. Soprano solo, female chorus, and orchestra. Words by G. Audigier. (1900.) Op. 114.

Le Feu céleste. Cantata for soprano, chorus, orchestra and organ, and a reciter. Words by Armand Silvestre. (1900.) Op. 115.

Lola. Scène dramatique à deux personnages. Words by Stephan Bordèse. (1900.) Op. 116.

La Gloire de Corneille. Cantata. Soli, chorus, and orchestra. Words by Seb. C. Lecomte. (1906.) Op. 126.
The Promised Land. Oratorio for soli, chorus, and orchestra. Text arranged from the Scriptures by Hermann Klein. (1913.) Op. 140.

SACRED WORKS

Messe Solennelle. Four voices, soli, chorus, and orchestra and organ. (1856.) Op. 4.
Tantum ergo. Chorus, with accompaniment of organ. (1856.) Op. 5.
Oratorio de Noël. Soli and chorus, with accompaniment of quintet of strings, and organ. (1858.) Op. 12.
Psalm XVIII., Cœli enarrant. Soli, chorus, and orchestra. (1865.) Op. 42.
Messe de Requiem. Soli, chorus, and orchestra. (1878.) Op. 54.
Panis Angelicus. Tenor solo, with accompaniment of quintet of strings or organ. (1898.)
Offertoire pour la Toussaint. Four voices, with organ accompaniment. (1898.)
Psalm CL., Praise ye the Lord. Double chorus, with accompaniment of orchestra and organ. (1908.) Op. 127.

Besides the above, Saint-Saëns has composed several settings of motets and hymns, such as " Veni Creator," " Ave Maria," " Ave verum," " O Salutaris," " Tantum ergo," " Inviolata," " Deus Abraham," " Pie Jesu," " Quam dilecta," etc. These include six settings of the " O Salutaris," five of the " Ave Maria," etc.

WORKS FOR ORCHESTRA

Symphony No. 1 in E flat. (1853.) Op. 2. Published, 1855.
Symphony in F. Unpublished. (1856.)
Symphony in D. Unpublished. (1859.)
Spartacus. Overture. Unpublished. (1863.)
Suite : (1) Prelude ; (2) Sarabande ; (3) Gavotte ; (4) Romance ; (5) Finale. (1863.) Op. 49. Published, 1877.
Rapsodie Bretonne. On the themes of the first and second rhapsodies for organ on Breton hymns. Op. 7. (1866.) Op. 7 *bis.*
Le Rouet d'Omphale. Symphonic Poem. (1871.) Op. 31. Published, 1872.

10

Marche Héroïque. (1871.) Op. 34.

Phaéton. Symphonic Poem. (1873.) Op. 39. Published, 1875.

Danse Macabre. Symphonic Poem. (1874.) Op. 40. Published, 1875.

La Jeunesse d'Hercule. Symphonic Poem. (1877.) Op. 50.

Symphony No. 2 in A minor. (1859.) Op. 55. Published, 1878.

Suite Algérienne : (1) Prelude ; (2) Rhapsody ; (3) Mauresque ; (4) Rêverie du soir ; (5) Marche militaire française. (1880.) Op. 60. Published, 1881.

Une nuit à Lisbonne. Barcarolle. (1880.) Op. 63. Published, 1881.

La Jota Aragonese. (1880.) Op. 64. Published, 1881.

Hymne à Victor Hugo. With chorus ad lib. (1881.) Op. 69. Published, 1884.

Symphony No. 3, in C minor. With organ. (1886.) Op. 78.

Le Carnaval des animaux. Unpublished. The melody entitled " Le Cygne," for violoncello and piano, is taken from this work and is published.

Sarabande et Rigaudon. (1892.) Op. 93.

Coronation March for King Edward VII. (1902.) Op. 117.

Ouverture de Fête. (1909.) Op. 133. Published, 1910.

Marche interalliée. (Jan. 1919.) Op. 155.

WORKS FOR PIANOFORTE AND ORCHESTRA

Concerto No. 1, in D. (1858.) Op. 17. Published, 1875.

Concerto No. 2, in G minor. (1868.) Op. 22.

Concerto No. 3, in E flat. (1869.) Op. 29. Published, 1875.

Concerto No. 4, in C minor. (1875.) Op. 44. Published, 1877.

Concerto No. 5, in F. (1896.) Op. 109.

Allegro appassionato. (1884.) Op. 70.

Rapsodie d'Auvergne. (1884.) Op. 73.

Africa. Fantasia. (1891.) Op. 89.

WORKS FOR VIOLIN AND ORCHESTRA

Concerto No. 1, in A. (1859.) Op. 20. Published by Hamelle, 1868.

Concerto No. 2, in C. (1858.) Op. 58. Published, 1879.

Concerto No. 3, in B minor. (1880.) Op. 61. Published, 1881.
Introduction et Rondo Capriccioso. (1863.) Op. 28. Published, 1870.
Concert piece. (1880.) Op. 62. Published, 1881.
Havanaise. (1887.) Op. 83. Published, 1888.
Caprice Andalous. (1904.) Op. 122.
La Muse et le Poète. (1909.) Op. 132. Violin and violoncello and orchestra. Published, 1910.

WORKS FOR VIOLONCELLO AND ORCHESTRA

Concerto No. 1, in A minor. (1872.) Op. 33. Published, 1873.
Concerto No. 2, in D minor. (1902.) Op. 119.

WORKS FOR OTHER SOLO INSTRUMENTS, WITH ORCHESTRA

Tarantelle. Flute and clarinet. (1857.) Op. 6.
Romance in F. Horn. (1874.) Op. 36.
Romance in D flat. Flute. (1871.) Op. 37. Published, 1874.
Morceau de concert. Harp. (1919.) Op. 154.

WORKS FOR ORGAN

Fantaisie No. 1. (1856.) Published, 1875, by Costallat.
Trois Rapsodies sur des cantiques Bretons. (1866.) Op. 7.
Bénédiction Nuptiale. (1859.) Op. 9. Published, 1866.
Trois Préludes et Fugues. 1er livre. (1894.) Op. 99.
Fantaisie No. 2. (1895.) Op. 101.
Marche religieuse. (1897.) Op. 107. Published, 1898.
Trois Préludes et Fugues. 2ème livre. (1898.) Op. 109.
Sept improvisations pour grand orgue. Op. 149.
Fantaisie No. 3. Op. 137.

WORKS FOR HARMONIUM

Trois morceaux : (1) Meditation ; (2) Barcarolle ; (3) Prière (1852.) Op. 1. Published by Girod in 1858.
Six duos. Harmonium and piano. (1858.) Op. 8. Published by Fromont in 1858.
Elévation ou Communion. (1865.) Op. 13.

CHAMBER MUSIC

Septet. Trumpet, piano, two violins, viola, 'cello, and double bass. (1881.) Op. 65.

Quintet. Piano and strings. (1855.) Op. 14. Published by Hamelle, 1865.

Quartet. Piano, violin, viola, 'cello. (1875.) Op. 41.

Quartet for strings, No. 1. (1899.) Op. 112.

Quartet for strings, No. 2. (1919.) Op. 153.

Trio No. 1, in F. Piano, violin, and 'cello. (1863.) Published by Hamelle, 1867.

Trio No. 2, in E minor. Piano, violin, and 'cello. (1892.) Op. 92.

Sonata No. 1. Violin and piano. (1885.) Op. 75.

Sonata No. 2. Violin and piano, in E flat. (1896.) Op. 102.

Sonata No. 1. Violoncello and piano, in C minor. (1872.) Op. 32. Published, 1873.

Sonata No. 2. Violoncello and piano, in F. (1905.) Op. 123.

Suite. Violoncello and piano: (1) Prelude; (2) Sérénade; (3) Scherzo; (4) Romance; (5) Final. (1862.) Op. 16. Published by Hamelle in 1866.

MISCELLANEOUS PIECES FOR DIFFERENT INSTRUMENTS

Sérénade. Piano, organ, violin, viola (or 'cello). (1866.) Op. 15. Published by Choudens, 1868.

Romance. Piano, organ, and violin. (1868.) Op. 27.

Berceuse, in B flat. Piano and violin. (1871.) Op. 38. Published, 1874.

Allegro Appassionato. Violoncello and piano (or orchestra). (1875.) Op. 43.

Romance, in C. Violin and piano (or orchestra). (1874.) Op. 48. Published, 1876.

Romance, in D. Violoncello and piano. (1877.) Op. 51.

Wedding cake. Caprice valse. Piano and strings. (1885.) Op. 76. Published, 1886.

Caprice sur des airs Danois et Russes. Flute, oboe, clarinet, and piano. (1887.) Op. 79.

Le Cygne. Mélodie. Violoncello and piano. (1887.)

Chant Saphique. Violoncello and piano. (1892.) Op. 91.

Morceau de Concert. Horn and piano. (1887.) Op. 94. Published, 1893.

Barcarolle. Violin, violoncello, harmonium, and piano. (1898.) Op. 108.

Fantaisie. Violin and harp. (1907.) Op. 123.

Elégie. Violin and piano. (1915.) Op. 143.

HARP

Fantaisie. (1893.) Op. 95.

WORKS FOR MILITARY BAND

Orient et Occident. Marche. (1869.) Op. 25. Published, 1870.

Hymne Franco-Espagnol. (1900.) Published, 1901.

Sur les bords du Nil. Military March. (1908.) Op. 125.

VOCAL WORKS

Sérénade d'hiver. Male voices.

Les soldats de Gédéon. Double chorus for men.

Two choruses (Victor Hugo): (1) Chanson de Grand père. Two female voices; (2) Chanson d'ancêtre. Baritone solo and male chorus.

Two choruses: (1) Calme des nuits; (2) Les Fleurs et les Arbres.

Two choruses. (1) Les Marins de Kermor: (2) Les Titans. Male voices.

Saltarelle. Male voices.

Les Guerriers. Male voices.

Madrigal. Tenor solo and male voices.

Chants d'automne. Male voices.

La Nuit. Soprano and female voices.

Romance du Soir.

A la France. Male voices.

Ode d'Horace. Male voices.

Le Matin. Male voices.

La Gloire. Male voices.

SONGS

Guitare. (Victor Hugo.) 1851. Published by Choudens.

Rêverie. (Victor Hugo.) 1851.

Le Pas d'armes du roi Jean. (Victor Hugo.) 1852.
La feuille du Peuplier. (Mme A. Tastu.)
L'Attente. (Victor Hugo.)
La Cloche. (Victor Hugo.)
Lever de la lune.
Pastorale. Duet. (Destouches.)
Le Sommeil des fleurs. (G. de Penmarch.)
Madonna col Bambino.
Viens. (Victor Hugo.) Duet.
Le Soir descend sur la Colline. Duet.
La Mort d'Ophélie. (E. Legouvé.)
Souvenances. (F. Lemaire.)
Etoile du Matin. (C. Distel.)
Extase. (Victor Hugo.)
Soirée en mer. (Victor Hugo.)
Alla riva del Tebro.
Canzonetta Toscana.
Le Matin. (Victor Hugo.)
L'Enlèvement. (Victor Hugo.)
Clair de lune. (Catulle Mendès.)
La Coccinelle. (Victor Hugo.)
A quoi bon entendre. (Victor Hugo.) Published by Choudens.
Le Chant de ceux qui vont sur la mer. (Victor Hugo.) Published
     by Choudens.
Tristesse. (F. Lemaire.)
Marquise vous souvenez vous ? (F. Coppée.) Published by
     Choudens.
Maria Lucrezia. (F. Legouvé.)
Mélodies Persanes. Set of six songs. Op. 26. (Armand Renaud.)
A Voice by the Cedar Tree. (Tennyson.) Published by Augener.
My Land. (T. Davis.) Published by Boosey.
Night Song to Preciosa. (I. Ginner.) Published by Boosey.
Si vous n'avez rien à me dire. (Victor Hugo.)
Désir de l'Orient. (Saint-Saëns.)
Dans ton cœur. (H. Cazalis.)
Danse Macabre. (H. Cazalis.)
Vogue, vogue la galère. (Jean Aicard.)
Dans les coins bleus. (Sainte-Beuve.)
Une flûte invisible. (Victor Hugo.)

Suzette et Suzon. (Victor Hugo.)

Chanson à boire du vieux Temps. (N. Boileau.)

Présage de la Croix. (S. Bordèse.)

Guitares et Mandolines. (Saint-Saëns.)

Amour viril. (G. Boyer.)

Aimons nous. (T. de Banville.)

Là-bas. (J. L. Croze.)

Madeleine. (A. Tranchant.)

Les Fées. (T. de Banville.) Accompaniment piano for four hands.

Fière Beauté. (A. Mahot.)

Le Rossignol. (T. de Banville.)

La Sérénité. (Mme M. Barbier.)

Primavera. (P. Stuart.)

La Libellule. (Saint-Saëns.)

Vive Paris, Vive la France. (A. Tranchant.) Published by Margueritat.

Pourquoi rester seulette. (J. L. Croze.)

Peut-être. (J. L. Croze.)

Vénus. (Saint-Saëns.)

Sonnet.

Si je l'osais. (A. Tranchant.)

Les Cloches de la mer. (Saint-Saëns.)

Thème varié. (Saint-Saëns.)

Nocturne. (Quinault.)

Les Vendanges. Hymne populaire. (S. Sicard.)

Elle. (C. Lecocq.)

Désir d'amour. (F. Perpina.)

L'Arbre. (J. Moréas.)

Le Fleuve. (G. Audigier.)

Sœur Anne. (A. Pressat.)

L'Étoile. (Prince Haïdar Pacha.)

L'Amour Oyseau. (Ronsard.)

Soir Romantique. (Mme de Noailles.)

Violon dans le Soir. (Mme de Noailles.) With violin obligato.

Angelus. (P. Aguétant.)

Où nous avons aimé. (P. Aguétant.)

Papillons. (R. de Léché.)

S'il est un charmant gazon. (Victor Hugo.)

WORKS FOR PIANO SOLO

Six Bagatelles. (1855.) Op. 3. Published, 1856.
First Mazurka. Op. 21. Published, 1868.
Gavotte. (1871.) Op. 23. Published, 1872.
Second Mazurka. (1871.) Op. 24. Published, 1872.
Romance sans paroles. (1871.) Published by Joubert in 1872.
Six Études. (1877.) Op. 52.
Menuet et Valse. (1878.) Op. 56.
Third Mazurka. (1882.) Op. 66. Published, 1883.
Album: (1) Prelude; (2) Carillon; (3) Toccata; (4) Valse; (5)
    Chanson Napolitaine; (6) Final. (1884.) Op. 72.
Souvenir d'Italie. (1887.) Op. 80.
Les Cloches du Soir. (1889.) Op. 85.
Valse Canariote. (1890.) Op. 88.
Suite. (1891.) Op. 90: (1) Prélude et Fugue; (2) Menuet;
    (3) Gavotte; (4) Gigue. Published, 1892.
Thème varié. (1894.) Op. 97.
Souvenir d'Ismalaïa. (1895.) Op. 100.
Valse mignonne. (1896.) Op. 104.
Valse nonchalante. (1898.) Op. 110.
Six Études. 2ème livre. (1899.) Op. 111.
Valse langoureuse. (1903.) Op. 120.

WORKS FOR PIANO, FOUR HANDS

Duettino. (1855.) Op. 11. Published by Hamelle in 1861.
Koënig Harald Harfagar, after Heine's Ballade. (1880.) Op. 59.
    Published by Bote & Bock, Berlin.
Feuillet d'Album. (1887.) Op. 81.
Pas redoublé. (1887.) Op. 86. Published, 1890.
Berceuse. (1896.) Op. 105.

WORKS FOR TWO PIANOS, FOUR HANDS

Variations sur un thème de Beethoven. (1874.) Op. 35.
Polonaise. (1886.) Op. 77.
Scherzo. (1889.) Op. 87. Published, 1890.
Caprice Arabe. (1894.) Op. 96.
Caprice Héroïque. (1898.)

TRANSCRIPTIONS, ARRANGEMENTS, FANTASIAS, ETC.

BACH, J. S. . . Six Transcriptions. First set.
" . . Six Transcriptions. Second set.
" . . Prelude of Sixth Violin Sonata, with piano accompaniment.
" . . Sarabande. Violin, with accompaniment of piano or orchestra.
BEETHOVEN . . Chorus of dervishes from *The Ruins of Athens*. For piano.
" . . Three Transcriptions from the Quartets for piano.
" . . Points d'orgue pour le concerto de piano en Sol.
" . . Cadenzas for the violin concerto.
BERLIOZ . . *Damnation de Faust*. Easter hymn. Transcribed for piano.
" . . *Lélio*. Score arranged for piano and voice. Published by Costallat.
BIZET . . . *Les Pêcheurs de Perles*. Scherzo. Transcribed for piano. Published by Choudens.
CHOPIN . . Sonata in B flat minor. Arranged for two pianos, four hands.
DUPARC, HENRI . *Lenore*. Symphonic Poem. Arranged for two pianos, four hands. Published by Rouart Lerolle.
DURAND, JACQUES . *Chanson des Maucroix*. Transcribed for piano.
DUVERNOY, A. . *Hellé*. Nocturne. Transcribed for piano. Published by Enoch.
GLUCK . . *Caprice sur les airs de ballet d'Alceste*. Piano.
" . . *Orphée*. Menuet. Transcribed for piano.
GOUNOD . . *Faust*. Kermesse. Transcribed for piano. Published by Choudens.
" . . *Faust*. Valse. Transcribed for piano. Published by Choudens.
" . . *Gallia*. Paraphrase for piano. Published by Novello, London.
" . . *Faust*. Kermesse et Valse. Transcribed for piano. Published by Choudens.

Gounod	. .	Suite Concertante. Arranged for two pianos, four hands. Published by Leduc.
Haydn	. .	Symphony No. 36, Andante. Transcribed for piano.
Liszt .	. .	Beethoven Cantata. Improvisation for piano. Published by Kahnt, Leipzig.
„ .	. .	*Orphée.* Symphonic Poem. Arranged for piano, violin, and 'cello. Published by Breitkopf & Härtel.
„ .	. .	*La Prédication aux oiseaux.* Legend. Transcribed for organ. Published by Rozsavolgyi, Buda-Pesth.
Lwoff	. .	Fantasia on the Russian National Hymn. Piano. Published by Leduc.
Massenet	. .	*Thais.* Concert Paraphrase. Published by Heugel.
Mendelssohn	.	*Midsummer Night's Dream.* Scherzo. Transcribed for piano.
Milan de Valence,		L. (Spanish composer, sixteenth cent.) Two fantasias for the lute. Transcribed for piano.
Mozart	. .	Andante. Transcribed for violin and piano or orchestra.
Paladilhe	. .	*La Mandolinata.* Paraphrase for piano. Published by Heugel.
„	. .	*La Islena.* Paraphrase for piano. Published by Heugel.
Reber, Henri	.	Four Symphonies arranged for piano, four hands. Published by Costallat.
Schumann .	.	Night Song. Arranged for orchestra or piano.
Wagner	. .	*Lohengrin.* Marche religieuse. Transcribed for piano, violin, and organ.

LIST OF COMPOSITIONS BY SAINT-SAËNS
PUBLISHED SINCE 1914

Op. 141. (No. 1) Des pas dans l'allée. Vocal quartet; (No. 2) Trinquons. Vocal quartet.

Op. 142. Hymne au travail. For four male voices.

Op. 143. Elégie. Violin and piano. 1915.

Op. 144. Cavatine. For tenor trombone, with piano accompaniment.

Op. 145. Ave Maria. For four voices.

Op. 146. La Cendre Rouge (G. Docquois): (1) Prelude; (2) Ame triste; (3) Douceur; (4) Silence; (5) Pâques; (6) Jour de pluie; (7) Amoroso; (8) Mai; (9) Petite main; (10) Reviens.

Op. 147. Tu es Petrus. For four voices.

Op. 148. Quam dilecta. Four voices, with organ and harp *ad lib.*

Op. 149. Laudate Dominum. Chorus.

Op. 150. Seven improvisations for organ.

Op. 151. Three choruses for female voices.

Op. 152. Vers la Victoire. Pas redoublé.

Op. 153. Second String Quartet in G. 1919.

Op. 154. Morceau de concert. Harp and orchestra. 1919.

Op. 155. Marche interalliée. 1919.

Op. 156. Cyprès et Lauriers. Organ and orchestra.

Op. 157. 3ème Fantaisie. Organ.

Op. 158. Prière. Violoncello and organ.

The following are without Opus number :—

Angélus. (P. Aguétant.) For tenor.

Où nous avons aimé. (P. Aguétant.) For tenor.

Papillons. (R. de Léché.) For soprano.

Vive la France. (P. Fournier.) 1915.

Victoire. (P. Fournier.) 1918.

God save the King. Translated and harmonized. 1914.

La Française. Chant héroïque de la Grande Guerre. (N. Zama coïs.)

Ne l'oubliez pas. 1915.

S'il est un charmant gazon. (Victor Hugo.) 1915.

Les Sapins. (P. Martin.) 1914.

Honneur à l'Amérique. 1917.

LITERARY WORKS

Harmonie et Mélodie. Published by C. Lévy. 1885.

Notes sur les décors de Théâtre dans l'antiquité romaine. Published by Baschet. 1886.

Rimes familières. Published by C. Lévy. 1891.

La Crampe des écrivains. Comedy in one Act. Published by C Lévy. 1892.

Charles Gounod et le " Don Juan " de Mozart. Published by P. Ollendorff. 1893.

Problèmes et Mystères. Published by Flammarion. 1894.

Portraits et Souvenirs. Published by Société d'éditions artistique. 1899.

Essai sur les lyres et cithares antiques. Published by Didot. 1902.

Le Roi Apépi. Comedy in four Acts, after Cherbuliez. Published by C. Lévy. 1903.

[1] *École Buissonière.* Published by Pierre Lafitte. 1913.

Au Courant de la Vie. Published by Dorbon-Ainé. 1914.

Germanophilie. Published by Dorbon-Ainé. 1916.

Les Idées de M. Vincent d'Indy. Published by Pierre Lafitte. 1919.

---

[1] Twenty-three of the thirty-six essays included in *École Buissonière* have been translated into English by Edwin Gile Rich and published under the following title : *Musical Memories,* by Camille Saint-Saëns. Published by John Murray. 1921.

BIBLIOGRAPHY

The following is a list of some of the works relating to Saint-Saëns. Except when otherwise mentioned, these are in French :—

EMILE BAUMANN . *Camille Saint-Saëns et Déjanire.* Published by Durand. 1900.

„ . *Les Grandes Formes de la Musique, L'Œuvre de C. Saint-Saëns.* Published by Ollendorff. 1905.

JEAN BONNEROT . *C. Saint-Saëns.* Published by Durand. 1914.

CAMILLE BELLAIGUE . *M. Camille Saint-Saëns.* Published by Durand. 1889.

FRANCESCO BERGER . *Reminiscences, Impressions, and Anecdotes.* Published by Sampson Low, Marston & Co. (Not dated.)

ALFRED BRUNEAU . *Musiques d'Hier et de Demain.* Published by Fasquelle. 1900.

„ . *La Musique Française.* Published by Fasquelle. 1901.

„ . *Musiques de Russie et Musiciens de France.* Published by Fasquelle. 1903.

ETIENNE DESTRANGES . *Une Partition méconnue : Proserpine.* Published by Fischbacher. 1895.

„ . *Samson et Dalila.* Published by Durand.

„ . *Consonnances et Dissonances.* Published by Fischbacher. 1906.

W. GANZ . . . *Memories of a Musician.* Published by John Murray. 1913.

CHARLES GOUNOD . *Henry VIII.* Imprimerie Chaix. 1883.

„ . *Ascanio.* Published by Durand. 1890.

„ . *Mémoires d'un artiste.* Published by C. Lévy. 1896.

157

GROVE'S *Dictionary of Musicians.*   Edited by J. A. FULLER MAIT-
LAND. Published by Macmillan. (English.)
1904.

ARTHUR HERVEY . *Masters of French Music.* With portrait.
Published   by   Osgood,   McIlvaine.
(English.) 1894.

„   . *French Music in the Nineteenth Century.*
Published by Grant Richards. (English.)
1903.

E. HIPPEAU . . *Henry VIII et l'Opéra Français.* Published by Imp. de Schiller. 1883.

HUGUES IMBERT . *Profils de Musiciens.* With portrait. Published by Fischbacher. 1888.

VINCENT D'INDY . *Cours   de   Composition   Musicale.* 2ème
livre. Published by Durand. 1909.

ADOLPHE JULLIEN . *Musiciens d'Aujourd'hui.* 1ère Série. 1892.
Published by *Lib. de l'Art.*

„   . *Musiciens   d'Aujourd'hui.* 2ème Série.
1894. Published by *Lib. de l'Art.*

„   . *Musique.*   Published   by   Fischbacher.
1896.

„   . *Musiciens d'Hier et d'Aujourd'hui.* Published by Fischbacher. 1910.

DAN. GREGORY MASON *From Grieg to Brahms.* With portrait.
Published by The Outlook Company,
New York. (English.) 1901.

JEAN MONTARGIS . *Camille Saint-Saëns (L'Œuvre-L'Artiste).*
Published by La Renaissance du Livre.
1919.

OTTO NEITZEL . . *Camille Saint-Saëns.* With illustrations.
Published by *Harmonie,* Berlin. (Ger-
man.) 1899.

FREDERICK NIECKS, Mus.D. *Programme Music in the Last Four
Centuries.* Published by Novello & Co.
1906.

ROMAIN ROLLAND . *Musiciens d'Aujourd'hui.*   Published   by
Hachette. 1908.

GUY ROPARTZ . . *Notations   Artistiques.*   Published   by
Lemerre. 1891.

GEORGES SERVIÈRES . *La Musique Française moderne.* With portrait. Published by Havard. 1897.

OCTAVE SÉRÉ . . *Musiciens français d'aujourd'hui.* Published by Mercure de France. 1911.

MYLES BIRKET FOSTER *The History of the Philharmonic Society of London.* Published by John Lane. (English.) 1912.

FILSON YOUNG . . *Mastersingers.* Published by William Reeves. (English.) 1901.

FRANZ LISZT . . *Letters* Collected and edited by La Mara, and translated by Constance Bache. Two volumes. Published by H. Grevel & Co. (English.) 1894.